LETTERS OF NOTE: DOGS

Letters of Note was born in 2009 with the launch of lettersofnote.com, a website celebrating old-fashioned correspondence that has since been visited over 100 million times. The first *Letters of Note* volume was published in October 2013, followed later that year by the first Letters Live, an event at which world-class performers delivered remarkable letters to a live audience.

Since then, these two siblings have grown side by side, with *Letters of Note* becoming an international phenomenon, and Letters Live shows being staged at iconic venues around the world, from London's Royal Albert Hall to the theatre at the Ace Hotel in Los Angeles.

You can find out more at lettersofnote.com and letterslive.com. And now you can also listen to the audio editions of the new series of *Letters of Note*, read by an extraordinary cast drawn from the wealth of talent that regularly takes part in the acclaimed Letters Live shows.

Letters of Note

DOGS

COMPILED BY

Shaun Usher

PENGUIN BOOKS

For all the good dogs, but especially . . .
Red, Claouey, Maydi, Lola, Liam, Luna, Buddy,
Holly and Darth

PENGUIN BOOKS
An imprint of Penguin Random House LLC
penguinrandomhouse.com

First published in Great Britain by Canongate Books Ltd 2021
Published in Penguin Books 2021

LIBRARY OF CONGRESS CATALOGING-IN-PUBLICATION DATA
Names: Usher, Shaun, 1978– compiler.
Title: Letters of note : dogs / compiled by Shaun Usher.
Other titles: Dogs
Description: New York : Penguin Books, [2021] |
Series: Letters of note.
Identifiers: LCCN 2021022628 (print) | LCCN 2021022629 (ebook) |
ISBN 9780143134749 (paperback) | ISBN 9780525506553 (ebook)
Subjects: LCSH: Dogs—Anecdotes. | Dog owners—Correspondance.
Classification: LCC SF426.2 .U84 2021 (print) |
LCC SF426.2 (ebook) | DDC 636.7—dc23
LC record available at https://lccn.loc.gov/2021022628
LC ebook record available at https://lccn.loc.gov/2021022629

Printed in the United States of America
1st Printing

Set in Joanna MT

CONTENTS

A letter is a time bomb, a message in a bottle, a spell, a cry for help, a story, an expression of concern, a ladle of love, a way to connect through words. This simple and brilliantly democratic art form remains a potent means of communication and, regardless of whatever technological revolution we are in the middle of, the letter lives and, like literature, it always will.

INTRODUCTION

The dog was the first animal to be domesticated by humans. In fact, we buddied up with the grey wolf such a long time ago that experts can't be sure exactly how many tens of millennia our friendship has endured. What is certain, however, is that our bond with 'man's best friend' is stronger than ever. Estimates vary wildly, but it is generally believed that there are currently in the region of half a billion dogs keeping humans company around the globe. And thanks to our refusal to stop meddling with nature, they now come in all manner of shapes and sizes: according to the Fédération Cynologique Internationale (World Canine Organisation), those half billion dogs can be divided into approximately 360 officially recognised breeds, ranging from your garden variety, no-nonsense players like poodles and Labradors, through to the lesser-known (at least to me, an ignorant Englishman) models such as the Norwegian Lundehund and the Hungarian Mudi. And we don't just keep canines around for companionship. On a daily basis, dogs are saving the lives of countless humans as they guide the blind, find bombs, search for missing people and detect disease. It is difficult to imagine life without them.

I write this on a Chewsday (forgive me) in November 2020, an undeniably terrible year now entering its 6932nd day. For hours, a gale has been thrashing the window behind my head and rattling the roof tiles above, the permanent low hum of radiators being warmed serving to remind me that the cruelty of winter is just weeks away. The political landscape is simply too grim to contemplate. Civil unrest seems omnipresent. In the UK we are in month nine of a life-changing pandemic that has already resulted in millions of deaths worldwide, devastation to the economy and the enforced isolation of huge swathes of the population. To put it bluntly, things are not looking or feeling great. And yet, to my right, curled up beside me, is Red, our permanently dishevelled dog. A ball of fluff whose very presence calms my nerves. A cherished member of our family who is blissfully unaware of any problems beyond our four walls, whose beautiful nature brings the very best out of our children and has taught them about life and love in ways we couldn't. It is no surprise to me that many of my fondest childhood memories star at least one of my family's dogs, and I will forever be grateful to my parents for bringing them into our home.

Despite all of the above, as far as I could tell —
and trust me, I have looked everywhere, even
beneath all the chairs — there did not already
exist a book filled only with letters related to our
trustiest companion. Certainly not in the English
language. Which brings us to the book in your
hands, *Letters of Note: Dogs*, a pocketable volume of
correspondence in which various people write
about, to or even through our canine friends. It
will make you laugh, cry and ponder our ever-
evolving relationship with this magnificent creature,
and maybe, should you not already be owned by a
dog, convince you to make the leap.

Fetch a drink, sit and let me lead you through
this epistolary canine treasury.

Shaun Usher
2020

The Letters

American writer E.B. White was born in Mount Vernon, New York, in 1899, and by the time of his death, aged eighty-six, he had truly mastered the art of storytelling. His children's novels include such classics as Stuart Little, Charlotte's Web *and* The Trumpet of the Swan. *White adored animals. According to his granddaughter Martha, he owned, at various points in his life, more than a dozen dogs that she knew of – many different breeds, numbering collies, setters, Labrador retrievers, Scotties, terriers and dachshunds among them. His letters, too, are littered with references to his four-legged friends, but none so charming as this one, written in response to an accusation by the ASPCA that he had failed to pay his dog tax and, as a result, was 'harbouring' an unlicensed dog.*

THE LETTER

The American Society for the
Prevention of Cruelty to Animals
York Avenue and East 92nd Street
New York, 28, NY

Dear Sirs:

I have your letter, undated, saying that I am
harboring an unlicensed dog in violation of the
law. If by "harboring" you mean getting up two or
three times every night to pull Minnie's blanket up
over her, I am harboring a dog all right. The
blanket keeps slipping off. I suppose you are
wondering by now why I don't get her a sweater
instead. That's a joke on you. She has a knitted
sweater, but she doesn't like to wear it for sleeping;
her legs are so short they work out of a sweater
and her toenails get caught in the mesh, and this
disturbs her rest. If Minnie doesn't get her rest, she
feels it right away. I do myself, and of course with
this night duty of mine, the way the blanket slips
and all, I haven't had any real rest in years. Minnie
is twelve.

In spite of what your inspector reported, she has

a license. She is licensed in the State of Maine as an unspayed bitch, or what is more commonly called an "unspaded" bitch. She wears her metal license tag but I must say I don't particularly care for it, as it is in the shape of a hydrant, which seems to me a feeble gag, besides being pointless in the case of a female. It is hard to believe that any state in the Union would circulate a gag like that and make people pay money for it, but Maine is always thinking of something. Maine puts up roadside crosses along the highways to mark the spots where people have lost their lives in motor accidents, so the highways are beginning to take on the appearance of a cemetery, and motoring in Maine has become a solemn experience, when one thinks mostly about death. I was driving along a road near Kittery the other day thinking about death and all of a sudden I heard the spring peepers. That changed me right away and I suddenly thought about life. It was the nicest feeling.

You asked about Minnie's name, sex, breed, and phone number. She doesn't answer the phone. She is a dachshund and can't reach it, but she wouldn't answer it even if she could, as she has no interest in outside calls. I did have a dachshund once, a male, who was interested in the telephone, and who got a great many calls, but Fred was an exceptional dog (his name was Fred) and I can't think of anything offhand that he wasn't interested in. The telephone was only one of a thousand things. He loved life — that is, he loved life if by "life" you mean "trouble," and of course the phone is almost synonymous with trouble. Minnie loves life, too, but her idea of life is a warm bed, preferably with an electric pad, and a friend in bed with her, and plenty of shut-eye, night and days. She's almost twelve. I guess I've already mentioned that. I got her from Dr. Clarence Little in 1939. He was using dachshunds in his cancer-research experiments (that was before Alexander Winchell was running the thing) and he had a couple of extra puppies, so I wheedled Minnie out of him. She later had puppies by her own father, at Dr. Little's request. What do you think about that for a scandal? I know what Fred thought about it. He was some put out.

Sincerely yours,

E.B. White

LETTER 02
MY FAITHFUL DOG MIGHT BEAR ME COMPANY

Frances Power Cobbe to *The Spectator*
18 November 1871

Frances Power Cobbe was an Irish journalist, feminist and dog lover who spent much of her life successfully campaigning for the rights of both women and animals. In 1892, deeply affected by gruesome stories of experiments being carried out on animals, she founded the world's first anti-vivisection organisation. Cobbe wrote numerous essays about the canine population, and in 1867 published The Confessions of a Lost Dog, *an autobiography 'written' by her beloved Pomeranian, Hajjin. In 1871, she wrote this letter to* The Spectator *in response to a recent piece in the magazine on Greyfriars Bobby, a famous Skye Terrier who for fourteen years, according to legend, stood guard at the grave of his owner in Edinburgh, awaiting his return.*

THE LETTER

Sir,

You ask in your last number whether "anyone can seriously doubt that Greyfriars Bobby has rejoined the master he loved so faithfully?" Pray allow me to state a reason which appears scarcely to have received the attention it deserves, for hoping that so it may be.

Admitting that many of the arguments in favour of the immortality of "the spirit of a man which goeth upward" do not apply directly to the spirit of a beast, it still holds, I apprehend, that if man's immortality be accepted as proven, a strong presumption may be thence derived in favour of the immortality of those creatures who *attain that moral stage whereat man becomes an immortal being.* What that stage may be we do not presume to guess, but we cannot suppose the tremendous alternative of extinction or immortality to be decided by arrival at any arbitrary or merely *physical* turning-point such as may occur at various epochs either before birth or at the moment of birth. We must believe it to be determined by entrance on some moral or mental stage such as may be represented by the terms Consciousness, Self-Consciousness, Intelligence, Power of Love, or the like; by the development, in short, of the mysterious Somewhat above the purely vegetative or animated life for which such life is the scaffolding. If, then (as we are wont to take for granted), a child of some six or eighteen months old be certainly an immortal being, it follows that the stage of development which involves immortality must be an early one. And if such be the case, that stage was unquestionably attained by the dog to whose honour Miss Coutts builds her fountain. To wait till the human mind and heart have displayed the intelligence and self-sacrifice of Greyfriars Bobby, before we treat children as immortal beings, would be, I fear, to postpone that promotion rather late in life for a good many of our little darlings.

I beg that it may be remarked that this argument expressly restricts itself to the case of the *higher* animals, and thus escapes the objection which has always been raised to the hypothesis of the immortality of the humbler creatures, namely, that if we proceed a step below the human race we have no right to stop short of the oyster. I merely contend that where any animal manifestly surpasses an average human infant in those steps of development which can be assumed to involve existence after death, then we are logically and religiously justified in expecting that the Creator of both child and brute will show no favouritism for the smooth white skin over the rough hairy coat.

Various authorities, theological and poetical, promise us in heaven harps, jewels, palms, and flowers, all sorts of good things from the vegetable and mineral world,—only, so far as I can learn, no animals except four monstrous creatures which few of us would desire to behold. For my own part, even if it betray a completely "untutored mind," I must confess that a world devoid of loving brutes and singing birds would seem to me wanting in a very large element of earth's beauty and happiness; and that instead of a crown and a harp, for whose possession I have no ambition whatever, I should be very thankful to find that

"United in that equal sky,
My faithful dog might bear me company."
I am, Sir, &c.,
PHILOZOOIST

LETTER 03
NEVER GET A BULLDOG
Roald Dahl to his mother
8 February 1944

When he wrote this letter to his mother, Roald Dahl was working at the British Embassy in Washington, D.C. – one of hundreds of undercover agents employed by Britain's MI6 foreign intelligence service to spy on the United States. Dahl's debut novel, The Gremlins, *had been published the year before, and it would be another seventeen years until his first children's book,* James and the Giant Peach, *set him on the path to becoming one of the best loved and entertaining authors in history. What is clear from his countless letters home during World War II, however, is that Dahl had been honing his craft for some time.*

THE LETTER

Dear Mama

I just got a cold; the first one that I've had for many months, since last spring, I think. There's not much point in telling you because by the time you get this, it will be gone – or I hope so anyway.

Last week a friend of mine in the embassy called Paul Scott Rankin went on leave. He left behind him for me to take care of, his enormous brown bulldog, called Winston. I said I didn't mind; he looked all right. But Winston is no ordinary old dog. He is stupid and lecherous and cantankerous and all the time he grunts and snorts and slobbers. Paul said, let him sleep in your bedroom and he will be all right. He snorts all of the time, but you will find that pleasant and soporific. So the first night Winston slept in my bedroom. He snored and grunted and made a great noise all night, and I slept very little.

In the morning I took him into the embassy and let him sit in my office. But he farted continuously and with great gusto. Once he did it whilst I was dictating to the secretary, and I had to turn him out on the spot so that she wouldn't think it was me. But he scratched on the door and I had to let him in again and open all the windows. He continued to fart regularly and contentedly for the rest of the day, and I was very cold with the windows open. Once when I went out of the room to see someone, I came back to find him sitting on top of my desk amidst piles of secret papers and red boxes which had G.R. in gold on their lids. I threw him off and he farted again.

That evening I had supper with crown prince Olav and Martha at the Norwegian embassy so while I went in I left Winston in the car. After dinner I said that I would have to go out and give Winston a walk and let him have a pee. They all said, 'Bring him in.' I said, 'He farts; he isn't any good and he has no respect for royalty.' They said, 'Bring him in.' So I brought him in and he spent the rest of the evening slinking around the room casting lustful eyes in the direction of the crown princess and belching quickly. He only farted once there, and they thought it was a Norwegian ambassador, so that was all right. The ambassador was embarrassed.

That evening I locked him in the kitchen. In the night he broke down the door, after relieving himself on the floor, and came rushing upstairs to the bathroom, where he shat hugely and decisively in the middle of my pink bathmat. I didn't sleep much that night either.

The next day at the embassy was very much the same as the one before. Then in the evening I was dining with Carlos and Maria Martins, the Brazilian ambassador and wife, so I took him in. Now Carlos Martins is a great connoisseur of food and wines, but with Winston lying underneath the table during dinner, he was not able to smell either the bouquet of the wine or the aroma of the food. He smelt only the smell which this wretched dog was making below. Carlos said after dinner, 'Winston makes much bad smell, eh?' I said yes he did, he was constipated. Then the next morning, completely exasperated, I took him to a luxurious and expensive dog's home and told them to keep him until Paul came back. Never get a bulldog . . .

Much hard work here.

Lots of love to all

Roald

LETTER 04
SHE'S NOT A BONE!

Lewis Carroll to Alexandra Kitchin
21 August 1873

*Alexandra 'Xie' Kitchin was born in 1864 to the Dean
of Durham, Reverend George Kitchin, and his wife,
Alice. From an early age, Xie – and to a lesser extent
her three brothers, Herbert, Hugh and Brook, as well
as her sister Dorothy Maud Mary – regularly sat for
portraits taken by an old school friend of her father's,
Charles Dodgson. Dodgson is better known as Lewis
Carroll, author of* Alice's Adventures in Wonderland.
*Carroll photographed all of the Kitchins, but it was
with Xie in particular that he shared a sense of
humour, as evidenced by this letter, written when she
was nine.*

THE LETTER

My dear Xie,

Poor, poor Hugh and Brook! Have you quite
forgotten that you've got three brothers? Why mayn't
they choose photographs too? I said "the children,"
you know. But perhaps you will say they are not
children, but that you and Herbert are the only two
children, and they are two little old men. Well, well,
perhaps they are: and then of course they won't
care about photographs: but they do look very
young, I must say.

The day after you went, I passed by your garden,
and saw the little pug-dog wandering in and out,
and it turned up its nose at me. So I went up to it
and said, "It is not good manners to turn up your
nose at people!" Its eyes filled with tears, and it
said, "I wasn't doing it at you, Sir! It was only to
keep myself from crying." "But what are you crying
about, little pug-dog?" said I. The poor little dog
rubbed its paws over its eyes, and said, "Because my
Ex—" "Because your Extravagance has ruined you?"
I said. "Then let it be a lesson to you not to be
extravagant. You should only spend a halfpenny a

year." "No, it's not that," said the little dog. "It's because my Ex—" "Because your Excellent master, Mr. Kitchin, is gone?" I said. "No!" said the little dog. "Do let me finish the word! It's because my Exie is gone!" "Well! What of that?" I said. "She's only a child! She's not a bone!"

"No," said the pug: "she's not a bone."

"Now, tell me the truth," I said. "Which do you like best? Xie, or a bone?"

The little dog thought for a minute, and then he said, "She's very 'bonne,' you know: that means 'good' in French. But she's not so good as a bone!"

Wasn't it an interesting conversation? Tell me what photographs Hugh and Brook choose: and give my love to them, and to Herbert: and take a leetle tiny slice of it for yourself.

Yours very affectionately,
C. L. Dodgson

LETTER 05
WHY NOT SEND AN ARMY OF BULL PUPS NEXT TIME?
Richard Richardson to The *Stars and Stripes*
August 1921

Born in 1916, Stubby the bull terrier was the official mascot of the 102nd Infantry Regiment and famously served on the Western Front for almost two years, during which time he stood guard for his human companions and even, on one occasion, held down a German soldier until back-up arrived. Stubby remains the only dog to be promoted to sergeant through combat. But despite his heroics, not everyone admired this dog. The following letter, written by an amusingly bitter war veteran, was sent to, and reprinted in, the Stars and Stripes *military newspaper.*

THE LETTER

Editor, The Stars and Stripes:

I see a big write-up in one of the newspapers of a dog that has received many honors and medals for his World War record. It doesn't strike me just right, and I'm writing this for publication just to show what one ex-soldier thinks of such a thing.

It is natural for a dog to follow his master, anybody knows that. Stubby followed his master to the front willingly no doubt. But did the dog have any idea at all where he was following his master to. No; and I'll say if he had he would have whipped his master and the whole company to keep from going.

But Stubby followed his master through the engagements some will say. Of course, he did, but what else could he have done? He was sneaking around with his tail tucked and wanting to run, but not knowing which way to run. He stuck with his master expecting him to see him through. For this Stubby gets all those medals and the name "a real hero."

But the thousands of real heroes, the red-blooded American boys who left gallons of their blood and maybe an arm and a leg on the battlefields don't get these honors bestowed on them. They didn't do anything to receive a medal or the name "a real hero." But a dog did.

If this Boston bull did so much and the boys didn't do anything, why not send an army of bull pups the next time and see who is entitled to these honors? I think the whole thing is nothing but a disgrace to the U. S. Army. I feel that I am insulted, and if every other American service man doesn't feel the same way about it I'd like to know what kind of tastes they have.

Maybe there is one or two in the world (there ought to be more than that) who think I haven't given the dog a square deal and that I don't look at the thing in the right way. If there is I would appreciate a letter showing me where I am wrong.

RICHARD L. RICHARDSON
Box 239, San Angelo, Tex.

LETTER 06
I'M STILL SOMEPLACE

Uncle Lynn to Peggy, Dorothy, Chuck and Dick
Jones
Date unknown

In his book Chuck Reducks, *the late Chuck Jones – a
legend in the world of animation, who created Wile E.
Coyote and Road Runner – credits his beloved 'Uncle
Lynn' with teaching him 'everything [he] would need to
know about animated cartoon writing' during his early
years. He also painted him as a hugely positive influ-
ence in his life in general and an 'ideal uncle' whom he
'worshipped'. Uncle Lynn also knew how to write. One
day, soon after the sad death of the Jones's dear family
dog Teddy, Uncle Lynn sent this heart-warming letter
to young Chuck and his siblings.*

THE LETTER

Dear Peggy and Dorothy and Chuck and Dick,
I had a telephone call last night. "Is this Uncle
Lynn?" someone asked.

"Why yes," I said. "My name is Lynn Martin.
Are you some unregistered nephew?"

"This is Teddy." He sounded a little impatient
with me. "Teddy Jones, Teddy Jones the resident
dog of 115 Wadsworth Avenue, Ocean Park,
California. I'm calling long distance."

"Excuse me," I said. "I really don't mean to
offend you, but I've never heard you talk before—
just bark, or whine, or yell at the moon."

"Look who's talking," Teddy sniffed, a really
impatient sniff if ever I've heard one. "Look. Peggy
and Dorothy and Chuck and Dick seem to be
having a very rough time of it because they think
I'm dead." Hesitate. "Well, I suppose in a way I
am."

I will admit that hearing a dog admit that he
was dead was a new experience for me, and not a
totally expected one. "If you're dead," I asked,
not being sure of just how you talk to a dead dog,
"how come you're calling me?" There was another
irritated pause. Clearly he was getting very impatient with me.

"Because," he said, in as carefully a controlled voice as I've ever heard from a dog. "Because when you are alive, even if the kids don't know *exactly* where you are, they know you're someplace. So I just want them to know I may be sort of dead, but I'm still someplace."

"Maybe I should tell them you're in Dog Heaven, Teddy. Maybe to make 'em feel—"

"Oh, don't be silly." Teddy cleared his throat. "Look. Where are you?"

"Oh, no, you don't. We're trying to find out where *you* are," I barked.

"Hey, I didn't know you could bark." He sounded impressed with my command of the language.

"Wait just a minute," I said. "You had to know where I am, or you couldn't have called me on the telephone, right?"

"Boy, you know so little," said Teddy. "I simply said I called you long distance. Who said anything about a telephone? They asked me if I knew where you were, and I said you were someplace else, besides 115 Wadsworth Avenue. So they dialed someplace else and here I am and here you are."

"Can I call you back?" I asked dazedly. "Maybe that'll give me a clue."

"Be reasonable," said Teddy. "How can you call

me back when neither you nor I know where I am?"

"Oh, come on, give me a clue," I begged desperately. "For instance, are there other dogs around there? I've got to tell the kids something."

"Hold it," said Teddy, apparently looking around. "I did see a pug/schnauzer with wings a minute ago. The wings could lift the schnauzer part of him off the ground, but the pug part just sort of dragged through the grass bumping into fireplugs."

"Fireplugs?"

"Orchards of them, hundreds of 'em. Yellow, red, white, striped. Unfortunately, I don't seem to have to pee anymore. I strain a lot, but all I get is air. Perfumed air," he added proudly.

"Sounds like Dog Heaven to me," I said. "Are there trees full of lamb chops and stuff like that?"

"You know," Teddy sighed. "For a fair to upper-middle-class uncle, you do have some weird ideas. But the reason I called you was Peggy, Dorothy, Chuck, and Dick trust you and will believe anything you say, which in my opinion is carrying the word 'gullible' about as far as it will stretch. Anyway, gullible or not, they trust you, so I want you to tell them that I'm still their faithful, noble, old dog, and—except for the noble part—that I'm in a place where they can't see me but I can see them, and I'll always be around keeping an eye, an ear, and a nose on them. Tell them that just because they can't see me doesn't mean I'm not there. Point out to them that during the day you can't see the latitudes and you can't really see a star, but they're both still there. So get a little poetic and ask them to think of me as 'good-dog,' the good old Teddy, the Dog Star from the horse latitudes, and not to worry, I'll bark the britches off anybody or anything that bothers them. Just because I bit the dust doesn't mean I can't bite the devils."

That's what he said. I never did find out exactly where he was, but I did find out where he wasn't—not ever very far from Peggy, Dorothy, Chuck, and old Dick Jones.

Sincerely,

Lynn Martin, Uncle at Large

'I'LL ALWAYS BE
AROUND KEEPING AN
EYE, AN EAR, AND A
NOSE ON THEM.'

— Teddy the Dog

LETTER 07
HOW I MISS HER
Anna Seward to William Newton
16 January 1791

Romantic poet and critic Anna Seward was born in England's Peak District in 1742 and was dubbed the 'Swan of Lichfield', the city in which she lived for much of her life. Seward remained resolutely unmarried until her death in 1809, living alone but for the company of her beloved lapdog, Sappho, named after the Greek poet born on the island of Lesbos. She wrote this letter to her friend William Newton shortly after the death of her four-legged friend.

THE LETTER

Jan. 16, 1791.

I write to you, thus early on the receipt of yours,
beneath the impression of a severe shock from the
sudden death, in my presence, of my darling
little dog, by the breaking, as is supposed, of the
aneurism in her throat, which had never seemed to
have given her the least annoyance till the minute in
which it destroyed her. Her life had been a three
year's rapture, so cloudless had been her health, so
gay was her spirit, so agile her light and bounding
frame, so pleasurable her keen sensibilities. How I
miss her, constant and sweet companion as she
was, it is not in every heart to conceive, or,
conceiving it, to pity.—Giovanni laments her not
less fondly; and her fate left no eye unwet in my
little household. Her loss has spread the gloom of
silence through this large mansion, so thinly
tenanted, that perpetually rung with the demonstra-
tions either of her joy or guardian watchfulness.
Her incessant affection for me, her gentleness and
perfect obedience, occur hourly to my remem-
brance, and "thrill my heart with melancholy pain."

My ingenious, learned, and benevolent neighbour, Mr. Green, whose poetic talents are admirable,

27

sent me the ensuing enchanting stanzas, the day
after I lost the beautiful, the clean, the sensible, the
beloved little creature.

TO MISS SEWARD ON THE DEATH OF HER
FAVOURITE LAP-DOG SAPPHO.

Cease, gentle maid, to shed the frequent tear,
That dims the lustre of thy beamy eyes;
Grief, and her tempting luxuries forbear.
Nor longer heave those unavailing sighs.

Say, shall that heart, with noblest passions warm.
Where friendship and her train delight to rest.
That mind, where sense and playful fancy charm,
By fond extreme of pity sink oppress'd?

What though thy favourite, with her parting
    breath,
Implor'd thy succour in a piercing yell,
And seem'd to court thy kind regards in death,
As at thy feet, in mortal trance, she fell:

What though, when fate's resistless mandate
    came,
Thy friendly hand was stretch'd in vain to save,
Yet can that hand bestow a deathless fame,

And plant unfading flowers around her grave.

Then let thy strains in plaintive accents flow,
So shall thy much-loved Sappho still survive;
So shall her beauties shine with brighter glow,
And in thy matchless verse for ages live.

Thus, if perchance the splendid amber folds
Some tiny insect in its crystal womb.
While its rare form the curious eye beholds,
The insect shares the glories of its tomb.

Severe has been the breath of this rugged
winter;—I hope it spreads no lasting blight in your
domestic comforts. I have been much out of health
through its icy progress, and obliged to throw
myself upon medical assistance. Within this month
my disorder has given way to the skill of my physi-
cians; but Mr. Saville, the disinterested, the humane,
still suffers seizures in his stomach, of an
uncommon, and surely of an alarming nature.
Heaven send they may be transient, and, in its
mercy, restore to health a life so valuable! Adieu!

WE NEED YOUR HELP
George Bush Snr to the White House staff
6 February 1992

Since 1800, when John Adams first moved into the newly built White House with his admirably named dogs, Juno and Satan, the majority of US presidents have brought their canine friends to live at 1600 Pennsylvania Avenue. In fact, Donald Trump was the first US president in over a century, since poochless William McKinley took the reins in 1897, not to own a dog. In 1989, when Ronald Reagan's Cavalier King Charles spaniel, Rex, left the presidential kennel, his place was immediately filled by Millie, the English Springer spaniel belonging to George H. W. Bush. Within months Millie gave birth to a litter of puppies, one of whom, Ranger, became Bush's favourite. In 1992, panicked by Ranger's ballooning weight, the president sent this urgent missive to all White House personnel.

THE LETTER

THE WHITE HOUSE
WASHINGTON

February 6, 1992

MEMO
IMPORTANT ANNOUNCEMENT
THIS IS AN ALL-POINTS BULLETIN
FROM THE PRESIDENT
SUBJECT: MY DOG "RANGER"

Recently Ranger was put on a weight-reduction program. Either that program succeeds or we enter Ranger in the Houston Fat Stock Show as Prime Hereford.

All offices should take a formal "pledge" that reads as follows: "WE AGREE NOT TO FEED RANGER. WE WILL NOT GIVE HIM BISCUITS. WE WILL NOT GIVE HIM FOOD OF ANY KIND."

In addition, Ranger's 'access' is hereby restricted. He has been told not to wander the corridors without an escort. This applies to the East and West Wings, to the Residence from the 3rd floor to the very, very bottom basement.

Although Ranger will still be permitted to roam

at Camp David, the Camp David staff including the Marines, Naval personnel, All Civilians and Kids are specifically instructed to "rat" on anyone seen feeding Ranger.

Ranger has been asked to wear a "Do not feed me" badge in addition to his ID.

I will, of course, report on Ranger's fight against obesity. Right now, he looks like a blimp, a nice friendly appealing blimp, but a blimp.

We Need Your Help—All hands, please help.

FROM THE PRESIDENT

[Signed]

George Bush

LETTER 9
THE ALL SEEING EYE
Morris Frank to Dorothy Harrison Eustis
9 November 1927

*Philadelphia-born Dorothy Harrison Eustis moved to
Switzerland with her husband in the mid-1920s, where
they would breed and train German Shepherds to
become police dogs. In late 1927, Eustis wrote a widely
read piece for the* Saturday Evening Post *in which she
spoke of a German effort to pair specially trained dogs
with blinded soldiers. The article provoked hundreds of
readers' letters, none so moving as this one, written by
a nineteen-year-old blind man named Morris Frank.
Eustis agreed to train a dog for the young man, and
five months later he travelled to Switzerland to meet
and bring home his German Shepherd, Buddy. Dorothy
Harrison Eustis and Morris Frank then went on to
found The Seeing Eye, the oldest guide-dog school in
the world.*

THE LETTER

Nashville, Tenn.
November 9, 1927

My dear Miss Eustis:
In reference to your article "The All Seeing Eye"
which appeared in the Saturday Evening Post of
Nov. 5th, is of great interest to me so that is the
reason why I take the liberty to address this letter
to you.

   I have often thought of this solution for the
blind but have never heard of it being put to a
practical use before, of course there are a few cases
throughout the United States realizing that if
handled in the proper manner and supervised
correctly this would be quite a help to the blind of
our country. I would appreciate very much if you
would be kind enough to give me more information upon this matter and if you would give me
the address of this school in Germany, or of any
trainer in this country who might have any thing
similar as I should like very much to forward this
work in this country, as three and a half years ago
at the age of sixteen I was deprived of my sight
and know from practical experience what rehabili-
tation means and what it means to be dependent
upon a paid helper who are unsympathetic and not

interested in their work and do not appreciate kindness as shown to them and as you well know that there are many throughout the land who not even have paid attendants.

I should like very much to be able to express my personal thanks and appreciation for the way in which you handle and put your message across. It touched those in my condition more knowing that what you said was near the real truth and I do believe that this gave the seeing public a very good idea of the situation and I hope it will help the public to come to a more clearer understanding as we do not require sympathy but a laughing word and a pat upon the back, kindly excuse me for rambling on in this manner but in my feeble way I am trying to give you the thanks you deserve.

Thanking you in advance for any information you may be able to let me have.

I remain sincerely yours,

Morris B. Frank

LETTER 10
HIS BARK, AS YOU MAY HAVE HEARD, IS TREMENDOUS
Thomas Dick Lauder to William Home Lizars
26 June 1839

Published between 1833 and 1843, The Naturalist's
Library *was a ground-breaking series of natural history
books edited by Scottish naturalist Sir William Jardine,
then printed and published by noted engraver William
Home Lizars. Its forty handsome volumes are dedicated
to different classes of animal, their pages illustrated
with drawings by various artists who were tasked with
bringing the natural world to life. The two* Dogs
*volumes are divided into breeds. Within the entry dedi-
cated to the mighty St Bernard can be found this
charming letter, written to Lizars by Thomas Dick
Lauder, a Scottish author whose dog, Bass, had posed
for the picture which accompanied the section in question.*

THE LETTER

The Grange House, 26th June, 1839.

Dear Sir,—My St. Bernard dog, Bass, whom you
have honoured so far as to have his portrait taken
by Mr. Stewart, was brought home by Sir Hew
Dalrymple of North Berwick, Baronet, direct from
the Great St. Bernard, and Sir Hew presented him
to me in December, 1837, when he was a puppy
of about four or five months; so that he may now
be reckoned about a year and nine months old. He
can hardly, therefore, be said to have reached his
full size. His bark, as you may have heard, is
tremendous; so loud, indeed, that I have often
distinguished it when in the Meadow Walk, nearly
a mile off. To it I was indebted for the recovery of
the dog when stolen by some carters, not long
after I got him. He had been some time missing,
when, to my great joy, one of the letter-carriers
brought him back; and the man's account was, that
in going along a certain street he heard his bark
from the inside of a yard, and knew it immediately.
He knocked at the gate, and immediately said to
the owner of the premises, "You have got Sir
Thomas Lauder's big dog." The man denied it. "But
I know you have," continued the letter-carrier. "I

can swear that I heard the bark of Sir Thomas's big dog; for there is no other dog in or about all Edinburgh that has such a bark." The man then admitted that he had a large dog, which he had bought for a trifle from a couple of coalcarters; and at last, with great reluctance, he gave up the dog to the letter-carrier, who brought him home here. But though Bass's bark is so terrific, he is the best natured and most playful dog I ever saw; so much so, indeed, that the small King Charles's spaniel lapdog, Raith, whom Mr. Stewart has also introduced into the same picture, used to tyrannize over him for many months after he came here from abroad. I have seen the little creature run furiously at the great animal when gnawing a bone, who instantly turned himself submissively over on his back, with all his legs in the air, whilst Raith, seizing the bone, would make the most absurd and unavailing attempts to bestride the enormous head of his subdued companion, with the most ludicrous affectation of the terrible growling that might bespeak the loftiest description of dog indignation. Bass has for some time ceased to tolerate this tyranny, having, upon one occasion, given the little fellow an admonitory shake; but he is at all times in perfect good humour with him, though Raith, from jealousy, is always glad to avail himself of an opportunity of flying at him. When a dog attacks Bass in the street or road, he runs away rather than quarrel; but when compelled to fight, by any perseverance in the attacking party, he turns upon him, throws his enemy down in a moment, and then, without biting him, he lays his whole immense bulk down upon him till he nearly smothers him. But this extreme softness arises from his youth; for if he were once fairly engaged, I have no doubt that he would be most formidable either to quadruped or biped who should venture to attack him. To give you an idea of his strength, I may tell you an anecdote which happened a good many months ago. He took a particular fancy for one of the postmen who deliver letters here, though he was not the man whom I have already had occasion to mention. It was the duty of the postman I now allude to, besides delivering letters, to carry a letter-bag from one receiving-house to another, and this bag he used to give to Bass to carry. Bass always followed that man through all the villas in this neighbourhood where he had deliveries to make; and he invariably parted with him opposite to the gate of the Convent of St. Margaret's, and returned home. When our gate was shut here, to prevent his following the postman, the dog always leaped a high wall to get after him. One day, when the postman was ill, or detained by some accidental circumstance, he sent a man in his place. Bass went up to the man, curiously scanning his face, whilst the man rather retired from the dog, by no means liking his appearance, and very anxious to decline all acquaintance with him. But as the man left the place, Bass followed him, showing strong symptoms that he was determined to have the post-bag. The man did all he could to keep possession of it. But, at length, Bass, seeing that he had no chance of getting possession of the bag by civil entreaty, raised himself on his hind legs, and putting a great fore-paw on each of the man's shoulders, he laid him flat on his back in the road, and quietly picking up the bag, he proceeded peaceably on his wonted way. The man, much dismayed, arose and followed the dog, making, every now and then, an ineffectual attempt to coax him to give up the bag. At the first house he came to, he told his fears, and the dilemma he was in; but the people comforted him, by telling him that the dog always carried the bag. Bass walked with the man to all the houses at which he delivered letters, and along the road till he came to the gate of St. Margaret's, where he dropped the bag, and, making his bow to the man, he returned home. I presume I have now given you enough of Bass. His companion,

Raith, is remarkable for having, in his eagerness to bark at some noise at the outer-door, jumped over a window twenty-three feet and an half high, on the hard gravel. He was stunned for a time, but he broke no bones; and, after about an hour's repose on his usual pillow in the large dining-room chair, he showed that he was as well as ever.

I am, dear Sir, yours faithfully,

THO. DICK LAUDER.

LETTER 11
SPOT
Zora Neale Hurston to Jean Parker Waterbury
15 June 1952

*Zora Neale Hurston was a prolific author and educator
whose written explorations of the African-American
experience led to her being referred to as the 'Queen
of the Harlem Renaissance'. Sadly, despite her early
renown, Hurston's achievements were largely forgotten
by the 1950s and she died in poverty in 1960, aged
sixty-nine. Hurston's final decade was spent in Florida
in the company of Spot, a black and white terrier
she adopted in 1950, and Spot's daughter, Shag. In
1952, Hurston wrote to her friend and literary agent
Jean Parker Waterbury with an update on an
ultimately unpublished piece about those beloved
furry companions.*

THE LETTER

Dear JPW:

Oh, I am so delighted over the award! You look so
very dignified in the picture receiving it for me.
Why, bless my soul! I could not have looked any
prettier my ownself.

[. . .]

I try to get down to work but it is hard now
when I worry about money. I think [that] at last I
have arrived at a good piece on SPOT. You have no
idea how much animal psychology I have acquired
in watching SPOT, her daughter, and the cat who
adopted me. I had no idea cats had so much intelligence. I have planned the piece out in a jointed
way. Each joint deals with some phase of my
observation. For example: 1. THE FELINE SENSE OF
HUMOR. Yes, I find that cats do have it. The
entertainment angle is much more important to
my cat than food. Incidents to illustrate the point.
2. THE THROW-BACK. Spot's daughter and her
reversion to the wolf. 3. THE VANISHED PUPPY.
Shag, Spot's daughter gave birth to seven puppies.
Two days later there were only six. The mystery of

the vanished puppy. Was Shag accusing Spot? The tense drama in the house between the two dogs for nearly two weeks. (I think Shag herself did away with the puppy. Spot sensed that she was being accused, and feared a murderous attack from her much larger and ferocious daughter. The scene when Spot, on the foot of the bed looked down into the slant, killer eyes of her daughter and trembled for her life in every fiber of her body. Me to the rescue. Myst[e]ry never solved.) Shag, the Wild but affectionate bitch. Scolded, she goes off, kills two chickens of a neighbor and brings them to me. 3. [sic] SPOT, THE MID-WIFE. 4. AMOROUS INCIDENTS. Observations on dog romance. I have proof that it can go further than the mating period. Spot is in love with a male dog, (owned by a city councilman) who has been castrated. Spot cannot understand his difficulty, but her loyalty to him is unabated. She will have no other. He lives a block up the street from us, and her tension, when she expects to see him, is tremendous. When he barks, day or night, she will run up there. She sits for hours in the drive looking that way. She has not been in heat for nine months. Sort of taken the veil in faithfulness to her eunuch. She will fight Shag or any other female dog who barks when her love barks. That is something that she alone must do with him. (Nobody can understand her behavior. It can only be explained under a romance such as humans feel.) 5. THE HOWLING KITTEN. A kitten, less than three months old comes howling strangely out of the dawn to the door. Both dogs and my own grown cat, name of Jean MacArthur Hurston, she is so beautiful and seductive, draw back from the howling kitten in some strange fear. All snarl at it, but none will get close enough to fight it. 6. THE IMITATIVE INSTINCT. Animal psychologists have stressed the fact that domestic animals do not imitate humans, but this is not true. Shag has tried to help me pick peas, tearing them off with her mouth. She imitates a human smile perfectly. A doctor studied her and said that it was not possible because dogs did not have the muscles at the mouth for it, but there it was. Both dogs and the cat help me to catch and kill moths and roaches that get into the house. Shag likes to lie on the window-sill. Seeing me run up the shade, she caught the edge of it with her teeth and tried it too. Spot tries to help me clean up by moving objects as she sees me do. Of course, she is likely to take one shoe to where it belongs, but jump upon the bed with the other one, or take it outdoors. 7. PUPPY-SITTING. Both dogs leave me in charge of puppies, and refusing to go out for a stroll unless I am there with the puppies. Evidences of perfect confidence, which they did not place in each other, of me left with their puppies. Indication of rapport and understanding. Jean MacArthur the same way. Has one kitten to which she is much devoted, but will leave it with me anytime. Allows me even to wash it. The humorous picture of the month-old kitten returning the favor, and attempting to give me a complete washing over with his tiny tongue.

I plan to do this piece in about 4,000 words, divided as I have indicated, under topical headlines.

Cow material still interests me if I can only stop worrying about money and get back to work.

It is hot here! The fish are going up and down the Indian river washed down in sweat.

All my love,

Zora

'YOU HAVE NO IDEA
HOW MUCH ANIMAL
PSYCHOLOGY I HAVE
ACQUIRED IN
WATCHING SPOT.'

– Zora Neale Hurston

LETTER 12
HE IS INFINITELY MORE THAN THAT
Helen Keller to Ichiro Ogasawara
1937 and 1940

*In 1937, as she embarked on a three-month speaking
tour of Japan, deaf-blind activist Helen Keller learned
of Hachikō, a famous Japanese Akita dog who, for a
decade, had returned every day to the spot in Tokyo
where he used to meet his long-deceased owner. Such
was her interest in the dog that when Keller travelled
home to the US, she was the owner of an Akita
named Kamikaze-go, gifted to her by a Japanese police
officer named Ichiro Ogasawara. Sadly, that dog died
at seven months of age. Keller soon wrote to
Ogasawara to break the news. Before long, the
Japanese government sent another Akita dog to Keller,
but she had no idea that the second dog had also
been donated by the same officer and was in fact
Kamikaze-go's brother. When she was finally told in
1940, she wrote to him again.*

THE LETTERS

7111 Seminole Avenue
Forest Hills, New York

November 19, 1937

Dear Mr. Ogasawara,

According to promise I am writing to you now, but this letter is very different from the happy one I was to have sent you. For I have some very sad news about darling Kamikaze. He died last night. It happened quite unexpectedly.

Kamikaze kept splendidly well during the voyage, and I am sure a more joyous young creature never lived. As soon as Miss Thomson and I arrived in America, we had him inoculated, so that he might have every chance of good health. He was thoroughly at home here. A weathertight, comfortable dog-house was built for him, and he stayed out-of-doors free and strong. He had a wonderful time playing with my Shetland Collies, lying in the sun or chasing the autumn leaves as they fell from the trees. His appetite was prodigious, we fed him on milk, vegetables, fish and meat.

But two weeks ago we noticed that he was not eating, and we took him promptly to the best veterinary on Long Island. The diagnosis was distemper. We could not imagine where Kamikaze had caught the germ, as he had never been away from our grounds. At first the doctor thought it was a mild case. He did everything humanly possible, giving him a transfusion, and serum injections, and we were sure that the puppy would be all right in a short time. But things have turned out differently, and another joy has gone out of my life.

How dear and loyal Kamikaze was! Every time I went out in the garden he would jump up to greet me with big affection. Nothing pleased him so much as to follow me round and round while I walked. I never saw such devotion in a five-months-old puppy. Whenever he was with us in a strange place, and Miss Thomson went out of the room for a few minutes, he would stick close to me. Once I shut the door, not knowing he was outside in the hall. I felt a loud noise and wondered what it was. Presently I learned that it was my faithful protector banging against the door and barking until some one let him in. He made friends with everyone, and all who saw him were enthusiastic over his beauty and his adorable ways.

Often I think gratefully of my visit to Nippon. My heart goes out to the people who were so wonderfully good to me, and upon whom such great darkness has now fallen. Sadly I consider how many sons and brothers they are losing in the war, and I pray that Buddha, the Lord of Light, may sustain them and point a way to renewed peace.

I will send you a photograph of Kamikaze which will say much that you can understand without a translation.

Miss Thomson, who also loved him very much, sends her cordial greetings with mine.

Sincerely yours,
Helen Keller

*   *   *

Arcan Ridge
Westport, Conn.,
April 1, 1940.

Dear Mr. Ogasawara,

Nearly a year has passed since I had the joy of welcoming Kenzan-go to my home. I wanted to write to you long ago and to send you a photograph of him in all his beauty, but not until recently was it possible to have the picture taken.

You will see that Kenzan-go is as handsome as ever and full of life, but he is infinitely more than that. He has become a splendid protector and companion, and is a precious part of my daily life. He lies beside me all golden in the sun while I write or read. Now and then he rises and lays his noble head on my knee with great affection. He is never so happy as when Miss Thomson and I take him out for a walk.

We have had deep snow-drifts here all winter, and it has been a delight to watch Kenzan-go rolling and leaping over them. Sometimes with a powerful paw he would break the ice in a brook for a drink, then away he would go, following the tracks of a fox or a deer in the snow, but he always came back telling me with nose, ear and tail to play with him.

It touched me greatly when I heard from Mr. Fleisher that you had given up your favorite dog for my sake, and he meant all the more to me. I thank you every time I stroke his beautiful coat or touch his tail waving like a pine bough in the breeze. I love him not only as your dog, but also as a message from the Japanese people whose friendship shines among my brightest memories.

With kindest salutations, and with all good wishes, in which Miss Thomson joins, I am,

Sincerely yours,

Helen Keller

LETTER 13
TRUST DOGS RATHER THAN MEN
Patrick Brontë to Charlotte Brontë
January 1853

In December 1852, the English novelist Charlotte Brontë
received a surprising marriage proposal from Arthur
Bell Nicholls, a man with whom she had no romantic
ties and who served as an assistant curate to Brontë's
father, Patrick, a priest. Patrick Brontë was shocked by
the news and furious, not least as he believed Nicholls
to be unworthy of his talented daughter. The ensuing
tensions resulted in Charlotte heading to London for a
month. This curious letter soon reached her, written by
her father in the voice of Flossy, a spaniel she had
looked after since the death of her sister Anne in 1849.
Brontë and Nicholls did eventually marry, in June 1854.
Patrick did not attend.

THE LETTER

January 1853

Flossy to his much respected and beloved Mistress,
Miss Brontë;
My kind Mistress, as, having only paws, I cannot
write, but, I can dictate—and my good Master, has
undertaken to set down what I have to say—He
well understands, the dog's language, which is not
very copious, but is nevertheless, significant and
quite sufficient for our purposes, and wants which
are not many—I fear that my Master, will not do
my simple language justice, but will write too
much in his own style, which I consider quite out
of character, and wrong—You have condescend-
ingly sent your respects to me, for which I am very
grateful, and in token of my gratitude, I struck the
ground three times with my tail—But let me tell
'to you' my affairs, just as they stand at present, in
my little world, little in your opinion, but great in
mine. Being old now, my youthful amusements,
have lost their former relish—I no longer enjoy as,
formerly, following sheep, and cats, and birds, and
I cannot gnaw bones, as I once did—Yet, I am still
merry and in good health and spirits—As many
things are done before me, which would not be

done, if I could speak, (well for us dogs that we cannot speak) so, I see a good deal of human nature, that is hid from those who have the gift of language, I observe these manoeuvres, and am permitted to observe many of them, which if I could speak, would never be done before me—I see people cheating one another, and yet appearing to be friends—many are the disagreeable discoveries, which I make, which 'you' could hardly believe if I were to tell them—One thing I have lately seen, which I wish to mention—No one takes me out to walk now, the weather is too cold, or 'too' wet for my master to walk in, and my former travelling companion [Arthur Nicholls], has lost all his apparent kindness, scolds me, and looks black upon me—I tell my master all this, by looking grave, and puzzled, holding up one side of my head, and one lip, shewing my teeth then, looking full in his face and whining—

Ah! my dear Mistress, trust dogs rather than men—They are very selfish, and when they have the power, (which no wise person will readily give them) very tyrannical—That you should act wisely in regard to men, women, and dogs is the sincere wish, of yours most

Sincerely – Old Flossy.

LETTER 14
SHE WAS ALL I HAD
T.H. White to David A. Garnett
25 November 1944

Born in Bombay to English parents in 1906, T.H. White is best known for writing The Sword in the Stone, *the first of four Arthurian novels in the series* The Once and Future King. *White's upbringing was fraught with difficulty and, according to his biographer, Sylvia Townsend Warner, his adulthood was marked by a profound loneliness. White's only true love was his Irish setter Brownie, and when she died in November of 1944 White's life fell to pieces. Distraught, he penned this letter to his agent and fellow writer David A. Garnett and sat with Brownie's body for two days.*

THE LETTER

November 25th, 1944
Doolistown

Dearest Bunny, Brownie died today. In all her 14 years of life I have only been away from her at night for 3 times, once to visit England for 5 days, once to have my appendix out and once for tonsils (2 days), but I did go in to Dublin about twice a year to buy books (9 hours away) and I thought she understood about this. To-day I went at 10, but the bloody devils had managed to kill her somehow when I got back at 7. She was in perfect health. I left her in my bed this morning, as it was an early start. Now I am writing with her dead head in my lap. I will sit up with her tonight, but tomorrow we must bury her. I don't know what to do after that. I am only sitting up because of that thing about perhaps consciousness persisting a bit. She has been to me more perfect than anything else in all my life, and I have failed her at the end, an 180-1 chance. If it had been any other day I might have known that I had done my best. These fools here did not poison her — I will not believe that. But I could have done more. They kept rubbing her, they say. She looks quite alive. She was wife,

mother, mistress & child. Please forgive me for
writing this distressing stuff, but it is helping me.
Her little tired face cannot be helped. Please do not
write to me at all about her, for very long time,
but tell me if I ought to buy another bitch or not,
as I do not know what to think about anything. I
might live another 30 years, which would be 2
dog's lifetimes at this, but of course they hamper
one very much when one loves them so desperately, and it is a problem. I am certain I am not
going to kill myself about it, as I thought I might
once. However, you will find this all very hysterical,
so I may as well stop. I still expect to wake up and
find it wasn't. She was all I had.

love from TIM

LETTER 15
TELL HIM TO WAIT FOR ME
Anaïs Nin and Rupert Pole
Spring 1960

In 1955, seven years after their first encounter, Anaïs
Nin married American actor Rupert Pole, despite the
fact that she was secretly still legally wed to first
husband Hugh Parker Guiler. With the husbands living
on opposite coasts of the United States, for many
years Nin maintained this unconventional set-up by
travelling the breadth of the country intermittently to
spend time with each. On the West Coast she shared a
spaniel with Pole called Tavi. Nin was in Paris when
the following letters were written after Tavi, already
deaf and partially sighted, had suffered a stroke.

THE LETTERS

My Love:

Quel jours! After wrote you from beach took Tavi to
McWherter's today (Monday after school) hoping he
could help but fearing he'd want to put him to
sleep. He's having same thing with his mother so
was very sympathetic—"Tiger" he called, but Tavi so
limp and listless and not like a tiger at all—but Mac
gave him another kind of injection (to "feed" the
brain) and said lots of cockers have lived through
strokes!! Said I could give him a little water after—
thank god as the ice bit was really getting me
down—also he can have a little ice cream to keep
up his strength—so I tore down to get some only
to find he didn't like it—but he does seem little
better today and is functioning normally (I take him
out and hold him up to wee wee). School is not
difficult—I'm just as glad to have him in the car
where he can't hurt himself.

Hurried home to fix things Reginald liked (he
called yesterday night late to say he had to talk to
me) then called him to find he was feeling much
better and thought he'd go down to Dorothy's and
wait for her to come home!!!

Sooooo threw out the last of the suki yaki vegetables in ice box (which had gone bad) and settled down to eggs, carrots, and the chipped beef which Tavi can't eat.

To relax decided to go to the Bergman "Brink of Life." Wow what a mistake—why didn't you tell me!!! Labor pains, abortions, death—went through it all with them as Bergman's actors always force you to do—how did he get those scenes?? And that was the actress on the operating table, not someone dubbed in. Even the second film (French) was hardly the relaxing kind—the hero—a wonderful man with liquid eyes and a mustache like Gil's— guillotined before the camera at end just after he finds his love!!!!!!

But all this—loveless marriages—children with no father—love aborted by the guillotine—only makes me realize more and more and more how very wonderful our love is—and how very precious.

That damn insurance thing you always send— always starts me thinking what life would be like without you—and each time I realize it would be completely lifeless—it would be no life at all—much worse than Tavi's life now—where he is at least spared pain—and thought—and of course he long ago stopped worrying about love . . .

61

But not his master—take *good* care of the master's love—and return it soon—unchanged.

Ever

R

* * *

Darling chiquito:

Your letter about Tavi upset me so much I was sad all day. Just before I left I whispered in his ear that he should wait for me and keep well. I had an intuition, and I wrote you about it—I was at Grazilla's and seeing her dog I worried about Tavi—I know what he means to us, yet darling, old age is so cruel it is better to not be alive—and the Tavi we knew lately was not the *real* Tavi. He has had much love and care—more than any dog I know. You know, he often wobbled to one side—he must have had a slight stroke before—I hate to think of Tavi being ill when I am not there to console you, to greet you when you come home. I hope perhaps it was a false alarm—and he may be all well now—I thought of you all day. Got your letter in the morning.

At 5 o'clock the English Book Shop started its

autograph party. All sorts of people came—old friends—new ones—writer, poets, Sylvia Beach, Harold Norse, Mellquist, an art critic who gave me introduction to biggest Swedish newspaper, etc. A Negro singer like Josephine Premice—painters, etc. We stayed until 9 o'clock. I was dead and hungry—then 8 of us went to dinner—small place. Fanchette got drunk and talked a lot of nonsense. 2 girls from Vienna who couldn't talk at all, then on to Deux Magots where I dumped them at midnight—too many people. I returned wishing to be in my little home with you—realizing more than ever I am made for intimate life—not public life. I'm tense and not happy with most people. I need the tropical warmth of my Acapulco marriage, life "a deux."

I hope I get another letter before I leave Saturday—The French never heard of Madrebon Roche [a drug]! I thought I could buy it cheaper here. It must have another name. I can get LSD from Jean Fanchette who is working at psychiatric hospital—perhaps.

Te quiero chiquito—love to Tavi . . . tell him to wait for me.

A

LETTER 16
HE IS MY SOLDIER
Francesco Petrarch to Matteo Longo
25 August 1351

Classical scholar and poet Francesco Petrarch was born in Tuscany in 1304 and, according to his voluminous correspondence, owned many dogs throughout his life. The first mention of any of these appears in a missive to a friend in 1338. When another of his canine companions died, he famously wrote an epitaph which read, 'Zabot, your house was small, your body was not long, and little is your grave, so take this little song.' In 1351, he wrote the following letter from France to his friend, the Bishop of Liège, Matteo Longo, concerning a dog of Longo's that Petrarch had adopted.

THE LETTER

Vaucluse

25 August, 1351

When you went away, your pitch-black dog, swifter than the wind, faithful beyond canine nature, "stood stock-still and moved not from the way," as Virgil says of Creusa. But the rest doesn't fit, for I don't think he "sank down, all foredone." No running, no obstacle, no steepness of the way could tire him who can, amazingly, seize a bird in flight and outstrip a hare. But such exercise is good for spirited creatures, while too much repose ruins them.

Being lost, no doubt, not recoiling from the journey but losing track of your course, and not knowing what to do in his distress, he would have gone to the woods to find his food—an easy matter for him—if Mother Nature had not interposed her law, that this animal does not live apart from men. Of all creatures under man's domination none is more faithful than the dog, as everyone knows, and none can be parted from man with greater difficulty. We know that some peoples used troops of dogs in battle instead of soldiers; and at need they did their duty very faithfully and never dodged the fight. We have read of some dogs who died for their masters, and of others who defended them vigorously and successfully from injury. Others, no less faithfully but less happily, served as guards until they fell transfixed, and not till they were destroyed was there any way to bring the masters low. Others survived their slain lords, and though cruelly wounded they would not surrender, and having failed to protect the beloved bodies from men's assaults they yet defended them in death from scavenging birds and beasts. Some avenged the death of their masters; others dug up with their claws the buried bodies, indicated with distressful barks the slayer hiding in a crowd and sank their fangs in the culprit and forced him to confession. Others, at their master's death, refused all food until they died. This happened not long ago in Padua, in the case of a very eminent man to whom in his life I owed much, and to whom I am still indebted after his life's end. After his cruel death, ever to be deplored, his dog, whom I knew well, so acted.

We have heard of some that clung fiercely to their masters' gravestones, and could not be dislodged until they died of hunger. Others jumped on their masters' funeral pyres and with them perished in the flames. Pliny the Younger and

Solinus tell a marvelous story, how the king of the Garamantes returned from exile by the aid of two hundred dogs who fought for him against his enemies. And there was a sad tale in Rome of a dog who could not be separated from his master and who followed him even into a prison cell; and when the master was executed the dog showed his grief by mighty howlings; and when people in pity offered him food, he would take it and put it in his dead master's mouth; and finally when the body was cast into the Tiber the dog jumped in and tried to bear the beloved burden to the surface, thus offering, as Pliny says, "to the multitude a marvelous example of animal fidelity." There are innumerable such stories of canine constancy, as I said before.

Hence, when you disappeared, where should your dog turn, since by nature he kept you ever in mind, shuddered at his empty life, and scorned to serve anyone else? The poor creature had only one recourse; he returned to his familiar home, where he had happily lived under your rule, whither he had often brought a blood-dripping wild goat or a hare, and had been awarded therefor your palm of victory.

But not finding any of your people there, he kept jumping wretchedly at your closed door, so that he wrung the hearts of all the passersby and filled us with regret for you. Then first we began to recognize our loss; we realized that you, whom we thought to be present, were far away. When the dog saw me he growled; but when I talked to him soothingly he soon wagged his tail and followed me of his own accord.

Now he accompanies me to the woods; he is my soldier. At my command he attacks wild creatures, and often brings me welcome booty. He is ready to come to you at your call; but he is happy in the meantime that good fortune has brought him to a friendly door.

Farewell.

LETTER 17
HE IS NOTHING BUT A LITTLE DOGGY
Clara Bow to Dobbie
1941

*Clara Bow was one of the biggest stars of silent film
during the Roaring Twenties – her meteoric rise after a
traumatising childhood was a true rags-to-riches tale.
But the sheer intensity of her decade on camera at a
time when celebrity culture was rearing its hungry
head resulted in burnout and an early exit. Fearing a
nervous breakdown in 1931, she and her soon-to-be
husband, Rex Bell, and her Great Dane, Duke, headed
for the Mojave Desert to live on a 400,000-acre ranch
far away from Hollywood. Before long, their family
unit expanded when Bow found an abandoned black
and white spaniel travelling a dusty path on their land.
She called him Diablo. Ten years later, with his health
failing, she wrote him this letter.*

THE LETTER

Little Dobbie,

Listen, I am saying this to you, as you lie asleep,
one little paw crumbled under your cheek and the
black curls stickily wet on your damp forehead.

I have stolen, stolen close to your crib alone.
Just a few moments ago as I sat reading, a hot
wave of remorse came over to me. I couldn't resist
it . . . guiltily I came to your basket.

These are the things I was thinking Dobbie . . . I
had been cross to you. I scolded you because you
jumped on me with your wet and muddy little paws
and ruined my favorite pyjamas . . . and stained my
new bedroom slippers. I spanked you for pulling off
the table cloth and breaking several pieces of my
coffee set. I called out angrily when I noticed you
had dragged some of my things onto the floor.

At breakfast I found fault too. You spilled your
food . . . you gulped down your biscuits in a hurry
. . . I lost my temper when I called to you and
there you were playing with King and not paying
any attention to my call and whistle.

Then it started all over again . . . this afternoon
as I drove in, I spied you digging holes in my
favorite flower patch – and they were holes alright.
If you had to dig, plant and buy those seeds you'd

feel the same way I did . . . and yet, why should I be so small about such petty trifles.

Do you remember later, when I was resting on the front porch watching the beautiful moon rise, how you came in softly, timidly with a sort of hurt, haunted look in your eyes? When I turned to you impatient at the interruption, you hesitated at the door. "What do you want?" I snapped.

You just looked at me, so sadly, then turned and ran towards me, jumped right on my lap and buried your cold little nose in my hands with such affection, which, God who is kind to all living, must have set blooming in your heart, and which neglect could not wither. And then you were gone, pattering into my room and crawled into your basket for the night.

Well, Dobbie, it was shortly afterwards, when, after reading awhile, the book slipped from my hands and a terrible sickening fear came over me. Suddenly I saw myself as I really was, in all my selfishness, and I felt sick at heart.

What had habit done to me? The habit of complaining, of finding fault, of reprimanding you. All of these were my rewards to you for being a little dog. It was not that I didn't love you; it was just that I expected too much of a little puppy. And there was so much that was good and fine in your little dog character. You did not deserve my treatment of you, Dobbie. The little heart of you was as big as the dawn itself over the desert hills. All this was shown by your spontaneous impulse to rush in and kiss me goodnight.

Nothing else matters tonight Dobbie dear. I have come to your bedside in the darkness and I have knelt there, choking with emotion and so ashamed. It is a feeble atonement. I know that you wouldn't understand these things, yet I must say what I am saying. I make a new resolve that tomorrow I will be a real pal to you – and more tolerant with you. When impatient words come I will bite my tongue and say – as if it were a ritual – "He is nothing but a little doggy!"

I'm afraid I have visioned you as a little human being. Yet as I see you now Dobbie, crumbled and weary in your little basket, I see that you are yet only a baby.

Dear little Dobbie, here on my penitent knees, I kiss your little curls – if it were not for waking you I would snatch you up in my arms and crush you to my breast.

Tears come, and heartache and remorse, and I think, a richer, deeper love, when you ran to me through the porch door and wanted to kiss me!

FINIS

'THE LITTLE HEART OF
YOU WAS AS BIG AS THE
DAWN ITSELF OVER THE
DESERT HILLS.'

– *Clara Bow*

HE PUT THEM ON THE RIGHT SCENT
Bob Hope to Fala Roosevelt
21 April 1945

*US President Franklin D. Roosevelt passed away on 12
April 1945 after suffering a brain haemorrhage. He was
sixty-three years old. Roosevelt had just begun his
fourth term after serving twelve years in the White
House, a record-breaking tenure, during which he had
led the nation through both the Great Depression and
World War II. Letters of consolation arrived from
around the globe, one of which was addressed to
Roosevelt's beloved Scottish Terrier, Fala, who had
become something of a celebrity during her master's
presidency. It was written by legendary comic Bob
Hope, in the guise of another dog named Fido, and
was reprinted in various newspapers. Fala remained
with First Lady Eleanor Roosevelt until 1952, when he
died. She is buried beside Fala's grave in New York.*

THE LETTER

April 21, 1945

Dear Fala,

You probably don't remember me. But I knew you
back in our kennel days when we were a couple
of young pups—in fact we chewed our first bone
together, remember? In writing you this letter, I'm
speaking for dogs throughout the world. For we
are all deeply grieved to hear of the death of your
master. Your personal loss is felt by all of us. You
know as well as I do that leading a dog's life is no
bed of roses. But a dog's life is for dogs. Human
beings shouldn't horn in on our territory. But
lately a lot of men and women and kids have
been leading a dog's life, and your master was
one of the humans who didn't like to see that sort
of thing happening. That's why we respected
him—he wanted to keep human beings in their
right place. And he did something about it. He
made plans, and people had confidence in his
plans because his integrity and sincerity were felt
the world over. In other words, he made a lot of
people see the light, or as we'd put it, he put
them on the right scent. Let's hope they can keep
their noses to the ground and work it out for

themselves, even though his personal guidance has been taken away from them.

With deepest sympathy,
Fido

LETTER 19
MY NICENS DOGSIE
Marcel Proust to Zadig
Shortly after 3 November 1911

It was in 1894 that French novelist Marcel Proust met composer Reynaldo Hahn. The pair instantly bonded through a shared love of literature and music, and their friendship soon blossomed into something more romantic. They wrote to each other regularly – Proust more often than not in a childlike language that could not have been further from that of the opus on which he was working, In Search of Lost Time. *In 1911, Hahn bought a black Basset Hound in Versailles, France, and named him after the Babylonian philosopher in Voltaire's 1747 novella* Zadig; or, The Book of Fate. *A few months after the dog's arrival, Proust wrote Hahn's canine companion a letter.*

THE LETTER

My dear Zadig,

I am very fond of you because you have a great
deal of chagrin and love through [the] same person
as I have, and you could not find anyone better in
the whole world. But I'm not jealous because he is
more with you as it's only fair and you are more
unfortunate and more loving. This is how I know,
my nicens dogsie. When I was little and felt sad at
leaving Mama, or going away, or going to bed, or
because of a girl I loved, I was more unhappy than
today first of all because like you I wasn't free, as I
am today, to take my mind off my misery, but shut
myself up with it, and secondly because I was also
tied up in my head in which I had no ideas, no
memories of books read, no plans which would
enable me to escape from myself. And you are like
that, Zadig, you have never read books and you
don't have ideas. And you must be very miserable
when you are sad.

But, my dear little Zadig, I would have you
know this, which as a kind of little dogsie like you
I can tell you and tell you because I have been a
man and you haven't: this intelligence of ours only
serves to replace those impressions which make
you love and suffer by faint facsimiles which cause

less grief and induce less tenderness. In the rare moments when I recapture all my affection, all my suffering, it's because my feelings have ceased to be based on these false ideas and reverted to something which is the same in you and in me. And that seems to me so superior to everything else that it's only when I've become a dog again, a poor Zadig like you, that I begin to write and books that are written like that are the only books I like.

He who bears your name, my dear old Zadig, is not at all like that. It's a little argument between your Master who is also mine and me. But you won't have any quarrels with him because you don't think.

Dear Zadig we are both of us old and suffering. But I should like to come and visit you often so that you bring me closer to my little master instead of separating me from him. With all my love.

Your friend

Buncht

LETTER 20
DASH IS VERY MAD INDEED
Charles Lamb and Peter George Patmore
June 1827

*For many years, the life of celebrated British essayist
and poet Charles Lamb was ruled by Dash, a large,
excitable, poorly trained dog given to him as a gift
by fellow poet Thomas Hood. Dash was a menace
who refused to be left home alone, resulting in daily
fourteen-mile walks that rendered Lamb permanently
exhausted and anxious, much to his and his wife
Mary's dismay. In September 1827, desperate to escape
with Mary, Lamb somehow persuaded his friend, Peter
George Patmore, to look after the beast until his
return from a short, relaxing break. Mid-trip, Lamb
wrote to Patmore for an update.*

THE LETTERS

Mrs. Leishman's, Chace, Enfield
June, 1827

Dear Patmore,

Excuse my anxiety—but how is Dash? (I should
have asked if Mrs. Patmore kept her rules, and was
improving—but Dash came uppermost. The order of
our thoughts should be the order of our writing.)
Goes he muzzled, or *aperto ore*? Are his intellects
sound, or does he wander a little in *his* conversation? You cannot be too careful to watch the first
symptoms of incoherence. The first illogical snarl he
makes, to St. Luke's with him! All the dogs here are
going mad, if you believe the overseers; but I
protest they seem to me very rational and collected.
But nothing is so deceitful as mad people to those
who are not used to them. Try him with hot water.
If he won't lick it up, it is a sign he does not like it.
Does his tail wag horizontally or perpendicularly?
That has decided the fate of many dogs at Enfield. Is
his general deportment cheerful? I mean when he is
pleased—for otherwise there is no judging. You
can't be too careful. Has he bit any of the children
yet? If, he has, have them shot, and keep him for
curiosity, to see if it was the hydrophobia. They say

all our army in India had it at one time—but that was in *Hyder-Ally's* time. Do you get paunch for him? Take care the sheep was sane. You might pull out his teeth (if he would let you), and then you need not mind if he were as mad as a Bedlamite. It would be rather fun to see his odd ways. It might amuse Mrs. Patmore and the children. They'd have more sense than he! He'd be like a Fool kept in the family, to keep the household in good humour with their own understanding. You might teach him the mad dance set to the mad howl. *Madge Owl-et* would be nothing to him. 'My, how he capers!' (One of the children speaks this.)

[German text, crossed out by Lamb]

What I scratch out is a German quotation from Lessing on the bite of rabid animals; but, I remember, you don't read German. But Mrs. Patmore may, so I wish I had let it stand. The meaning in English is—'Avoid to approach an animal suspected of madness, as you would avoid fire or a precipice:'—which I think is a sensible observation. The Germans are certainly profounder than we.

If the slightest suspicion arises in your breast, that all is not right with him (Dash), muzzle him, and lead him in a string (common pack-thread will do; he don't care for twist) to Hood's, his quondam master, and he'll take him in at any time.

You may mention your suspicion or not, as you like, or as you think it may wound or not Mr. H's feelings. Hood, I know, will wink at a few follies in Dash, in consideration of his former sense. Besides, Hood is deaf, and if you hinted anything, ten to one he would not hear you. Besides, you will have discharged your conscience, and laid the child at the right door, as they say.

We are dawdling our time away very idly and pleasantly, at a Mrs Leishman's, Chace, Enfield, where, if you come a-hunting, we can give you cold meat and a tankard. Her husband is a tailor; but that, you know, does not make her one. I knew a jailor (which rhymes), but his wife was a fine lady.

Let us hear from you respecting Mrs. Patmore's regimen. I send my love in a —— to Dash.

C. Lamb

* * *

Dear Lamb,

Dash is very mad indeed. As I knew you would be shocked to hear it, I did not volunteer to trouble your peaceful retreat by the sad information, thinking it could do no good, either to you, to Dash, to us, or to the innocent creature that he has already bitten, or to those he may (please God) bite hereafter. But when you ask it of me as a friend, I cannot withhold the truth from you. The poor little patient has resolutely refused to touch water (either hot or cold) ever since, and if we attempt to force it down her throat, she scratches, grins, fights, makes faces, and utters strange noises, showing every recognised symptom of being very mad indeed . . .

As for your panacea (of shooting the bitten one), we utterly set our faces against it, not thinking death 'a happy release' under any given circumstances, and being specially averse to it under circumstances given by our own neglect.

By the bye, it has just occurred to me, that the fact of the poor little sufferer making a noise more like a cat's than a dog's, may possibly indicate that she is not quite so mad as we at first feared. Still there is no saying but the symptom may be one of aggravation. Indeed I shouldn't wonder if the 'faculty' preferred the bark, as that (under the queer name of quinine) has been getting very fashionable among them of late.

I wish you could have seen the poor little patient before we got rid of her—how she scoured round the kitchen among the pots and pans, scampered about the garden, and clambered to the tops of the highest trees. (No symptoms of high-drophobia, you will say, in that.) . . .

By the bye again, I have entirely forgotten to tell you, that the injured innocent is not one of our children, but of the cat's; and this reminds me to tell you that, putting cats out of the question (to which, like some of his so-called 'betters,' Dash has evidently a 'natural antipathy'), he comports himself in all other respects as a sane and well-bred dog should do. In fact, his distemper, I am happy to tell you, is clearly not insanity, but only a temporary hallucination or monomania in regard (want of regard, you will say) to one particular species of his fellow-creatures—*videlicet*, cats. (For the delicate distinctions in these cases, see Hazlem *passim*; or pass him, if you prefer it.) . . .

With respect to the second subject of your kind inquiries—the lady, and the success of her prescribed regimen—I will not say that she absolutely *barks* at the sight of water when proffered to her, but she shakes her head, and sighs piteously, which are bad symptoms. In sober seriousness, her watery regimen does not yet show any signs of doing her good, and we have now finally determined on going to France for the summer, and shall leave North End, with that purpose, in about three weeks.

I was going up to Colnbrook Cottage on the very Monday that you left; but (for a wonder) I took the precaution of calling on your ancient friend at the factory in my way, and learned that you had left . . .

I hope you will not feel yourselves justified in remaining long at Enfield, for if you do, I shall certainly devise some means of getting down to see you, in which case I shall inevitably stay very late at night, and in all human probability shall be stopped and robbed in coming back; so that your sister, if not you, will see the propriety of your returning to town as soon as may be.

Talking of being stopped on the King's Highway, reminds me of Dash's last exploit. He was out at near dusk, down the lane, a few nights ago, with his mistress (who is as fond of him as his master— please to be careful how you construe this last equivocally expressed phrase, and don't make the 'master' an accusative case), when Dash attacked a carpenter armed with a large saw—not Dash, but the carpenter—and a 'wise saw' it turned out, for its teeth protected him from Dash's, and a battle royal ensued, worthy the Surrey theatre. Mrs. Patmore says that it was really frightful to see the saw, and the way in which it and Dash gnashed their teeth at each other . . .

Ever yours,

P. G. P.

LETTER 21
A LOVELY LETTER ABOUT BASKET
Gertrude Stein to Alexander Woollcott
December 1935

*Iconic modernist novelist and poet Gertrude Stein
adored dogs – so much so that she and her partner,
Alice B. Toklas, owned, at various points, multiple
Chihuahuas and three white poodles in succession, all
named Basket. This passion was also shared by the
couple's friend, the noted critic Alexander Woollcott,
and, as 1935 came to a close, she wrote to him with an
update on Basket number one, a supremely pampered
dog she and Toklas bought at a Paris dog show in 1929
and bathed in sulphur water each morning.*

THE LETTER

27 rue de Fleurus
Paris.

My dear friend
I want to tell you all about Basket, but first how
touched I was by your story, it was a lovely story,
and a beautiful to me finish to the war story of the
Lonesome Pine, one's biography by song is interesting, when young adolescence dreamed in A
Spanish cavalier stood on his retreat and on his
guitar played a tune love, and my medical school
was accompanied by And the moon was shining
bright upon the Wabash and the moon was shining
bright upon the sea, the men used to croon that
while we worked, and in the public schools it used
to be come with thy lute to the fountain sing me a
song of the mountain, and I have no idea who
wrote any of them either words or music, but you
will know, and that too is a most enormous
pleasure, but I want to tell you about Basket, Basket
did one thing that was lovely when we came back
from the country he had no basket in which to
sleep, he has one in the country and he had one
here but when we left him and his basket when we
were in America he was so miserable that he tore

his basket all up, so when we got to Paris I put down a blanket and he slept on it not too unhappily and then after a couple of days one day while I happened to look at him he deliberately tried to fit himself into the little Mexican dog's basket, he solemnly tried he protruded first one side and then the other never looking at me but solemnly trying to fit himself into the tiny basket, it was one of the most comical and one of the most reproachful things I have ever seen, of course I immediately took him out and bought him a basket, the matter has never again been mentioned between us, I think I told you that once when Basket was playing with his ball, by the way Basket's vocabulary all goes with b. he has bed and basket, and beg and bone and ball, he only talks in bs well the little Mexican got Basket's ball and sat on it and I looked up and there was Basket making the beau sitting up and begging for the ball, the little Mexican looked up at him as if he had gone mad and went on chasing the ball, for the first time in his life Basket had sat up and begged and not gotten what he asked he was disillusioned and there were tears in his eyes he has never been quite the same trusting dog since, he is a darling and I do hope someday you and he will meet, he is perhaps too friendly he errs on that side, and even when another dog bites

him, he is convinced that it was an accident, he
cannot accept it as intentional, he keeps his spirit
pure and even when the little lambs in the village
follow him because they think he is a sheep and
the mother sheep butts him because she thinks he
is leading off her babies to destroy them, he is just
surprised. He only barks when the little Mexican
tells him to, and he also only chases chickens when
the little one leads the way, in short he is a happy
fool, and a great comfort, and some day you will
meet, there have I written you a lovely letter about
Basket, there he is all white on the rug and sends
you his best, merriest of merry Christmases as you
are giving every one

Always and always
Gtde Stein

'[E]VEN WHEN
ANOTHER DOG
BITES HIM, HE IS
CONVINCED IT WAS AN
ACCIDENT . . .'

– Gertrude Stein

LETTER 22
YOUR HIGHNESSE WOULD LOVE MY DOGGE
Sir John Harington to Prince Henry
14 June 1608

Sir John Harington had many strings to his bow: he was an author, a poet, a translator, a courtier to Queen Elizabeth I, and the inventor of the modern flushing toilet. He was also a devoted dog lover and proud owner of a pale brown spaniel named Bungey. In 1608, Bungey died, resulting in this letter to the son of King James I, Prince Henry, who was a friend and hunting companion. In it, along with news of his dog's recent death, he details at some length the tricks his intelligent dog was able to perform and recalls the time Bungey was dognapped, leading to a rescue attempt by Harington involving a pheasant.

THE LETTER

May it please your Highnesse to accept in as good
sorte what I nowe offer, as hath been done afore-
tyme; and I may saie, I *pede fausto* [go with a lucky
foot]: but, havinge goode reason to thinke your
Highnesse had goode will and likinge to reade
what others have tolde of my rare dogge, I will
even give a brief historie of his good deedes and
straunge feats; and herein will I not plaie the curr
myselfe, but in goode soothe relate what is not
more nor lesse than bare verity. Althowgh I mean
not to disparage the deeds of Alexander's horse, I
will match my dogge against him for good
carriage, for, if he did not bear a great *Prince* on his
back, I am bolde to saie he did often bear the
sweet wordes of a greater *Princesse* on his necke.

I did once relate to your Highnesse after what
sorte his tacklinge was wherewithe he did sojourn
from my house at the Bathe to Greenwiche Palace,
and deliver up to the cowrte there such matters as
were entrusted to his care. This he hathe often
done, and came safe to the Bathe, or my house
here at Kelstone, with goodlie returnes from such
nobilitie as were pleasede to emploie him; nor was
it ever tolde our Ladie Queene that the messenger
did ever blab ought concerninge his highe truste,

as others have done in more special matters.
Neither must it be forgotten, as how he once was
sente with two charges of sack wine from the
Bathe to my howse, by my man Combe; and on his
way the cordage did slackene; but my trustie bearer
did now bear himselfe so wisely as to covertly hide
one flasket in the rushes, and take the other in his
teethe to the howse; after whiche he went forthe,
and returnede with the other parte of his burden to
dinner. Hereat your Highnesse may perchance
marvele and doubte; but we have livinge testimonie
of those who wroughte in the fieldes, and espiede
his worke, and now live to tell that they did muche
longe to plaie the dogge, and give stowage of the
wine to themselves; but they did refrain, and
watchede the passinge of this whole business.

I neede not saie how muche I did once grieve at
missinge this dogge; for, on my journie towardes
Londonne, some idle pastimers did diverte themselves with huntinge mallards in a ponde, and
conveyd him to the Spanish ambassadors, where (in
a happie houre) after six weeks I did heare of him,
but suche was the cowrte he did pay to the Don,
that he was no lesse in good likinge there than at
home. Nor did the householde listen to my claim,
or challenge, till I rested my suite on the dogges
own proofes, and made him performe such feats

before the nobles assembled, as put it past doubt that I was his master. I did send him to the hall in the time of dinner, and made him bring thence a pheasant out the dish, which created much mirthe; but much more, when he returnede atte my commandment to the table, and put it again in the same cover. Herewith the companie was well content to allow me my claim, and we bothe were well content to accepte it, and came homewardes.

I could dwell more on this matter, but *jubes renovare dolorem* [too cruel is the pain]. I will now saie in what manner he died. As we traveld towardes the Bathe, he leapede on my horses necke, and was more earneste in fawninge and courtinge my notice, than what I had observed for time backe; and, after my chidinge his disturbinge my passinge forwardes, he gave me some glances of such affection as moved me to cajole him; but alas! he crept suddenly into a thorny brake, and died in a short time.

Thus I have strove to rehearse such of his deedes as maie suggest much more to your Highnesse thought of this dogge. But having saide so much of him in prose, I will say somewhat too in verse, as you may finde hereafter at the close of the historie. Now let Ulysses praise his dogge Argus, or Tobite be led by that dogge whose name doth not appear;

yet could I say such things of my *Bungey*, (for so was he styled), as might shame them both, either for good faith, clear wit, or wonderful deedes; to say no more than I have said, of his bearing letters to London and Greenwiche, more than a hundred miles. As I doubt not but your Highnesse would love my dogge, if not myselfe, I have been thus tedious in his storie; and again saie, that of all the dogges near your father's courte not one hathe more love, more diligence to please, or less pay for pleasinge, than him I write of; for verily a bone would contente my servante, when some expecte great matters, or will knavishly find oute a bone of contention.

I nowe reste your Highnesse friend, in all service that maye suite him,

John Harington

LETTER 23
HE LOOKED SO BEAUTIFUL
Georgia O'Keeffe to Todd Webb
20 November 1981

*Following the death of her husband Alfred Stieglitz, in
1946, pioneering American artist Georgia O'Keeffe relo-
cated from New York to the place which for years had
inspired many of her paintings: Abiquiú, New Mexico.
It was there, in 1953, that O'Keeffe fell in love with the
Chow Chow, a sturdy, black-tongued, thick-furred dog
originating in China and of which her neighbour,
Richard Pritzlaff, was a breeder. O'Keeffe would go on
to own at least seven Chows, all of which she referred
to as 'little people'. Her first two were Bo and Chia.
Sadly, Bo, her favourite, died at the age of three after
being hit by a truck, and the experience remained on
O'Keeffe's mind for the rest of her life. In 1981, she wrote
this letter to Todd Webb, a celebrated photographer and
friend.*

THE LETTER

[Abiquiú]
November 20, 1981

Dear Todd:

It was good to see you and have coffee with you
early in the morning — a little after six — even
though it wasn't orderly.

I have wanted to remind you of what you did
for me years ago and thank you. [. . .]

As you may know, Richard thought I ought to
have a dog so from a new litter of his puppies he
gave me one. It was lavender like a Maltese cat
with tail and back hair almost white. I had quite a
time to get that dog to be mine and didn't really
accept that. I took him to the ranch — fed him
myself and walked him out toward the cliffs —
morning and evenings. It got so that I reached
home first and blew my whistle — it was one of
those whistles that you can hear for a mile. He
would come running like a bullet to me. He was
big with a strong smooth coat and when he was
in Abiquiú he was the town boss. At that time my
dogs were free to run around the town from 6
A.M. to 6 P.M. He had some bad scars from the
fights that made him the town boss. He would run

through a flock of chickens as if they were not there.

One morning he came in the back way — dragging his legs behind him. There was much excitement and you came out. We called the vet who came immediately. When he saw that the dog could not move those legs, he said, "We will see before we do anything else. Keep him for two weeks, and see if he can move his legs." I was really completely upset, so every morning at the first sight of dawn, I got up and went out to look at the dog and talk to him

When the two weeks were up, there was a very very slight movement in the tail — almost nothing. So again I called the vet. As he looked the dog over, he said that it would be hard for the dog to drag those legs always. — You were there — We talked a little and decided to put him to sleep and call it his end. He had had a good life. He looked so beautiful as he sat there with us. When I think of it now I even get an odd feeling in my stomach. He was given a shot and lay quietly down. He was put in the back of the car. It was all that a man could do to lift him in.

We drove out into the White Hills — dug a hole under a small sized cedar bush and put my beautiful dog into it and covered him with earth and many rocks. I like to think that probably he goes running and leaping through the White Hills alone in the night.

The photographs came — for which thanks. I am sending you some writing, I hope it is what you want

Sincerely,

Georgia O'Keeffe

'I LIKE TO THINK THAT
PROBABLY HE GOES
RUNNING AND LEAPING
THROUGH THE WHITE
HILLS ALONE IN THE
NIGHT.'

— Georgia O'Keeffe

LETTER 24
I HOPE YOU WERE GOING SOME PLACE IMPORTANT

Richard Joseph to the man who killed his dog
August 1955

In 1955, travel editor Richard Joseph and his wife,
Morgan, escaped the intensity of New York and moved
to the relative peace and quiet of Connecticut. Having
quickly adjusted to this new pace of life, they bought a
young Basset Hound named Vicky. One Tuesday
evening tragedy struck when a speeding car veered
into their new pet as Richard took her for a walk,
killing her almost instantly. The driver fled the scene.
On Wednesday morning Richard wrote this letter to
the local newspaper, the Westport Town Crier and
Herald, *hoping it would be printed. The next day*
Johnson's letter was on the paper's front page; it was
then reprinted in dozens of newspapers across the US.
In 1957, it inspired a book. The driver of the car
remained unknown.

THE LETTER

I hope you were going some place important when
you drove so fast down Cross Highway across
Bayberry Lane, Tuesday night.

I hope that when you got there the time you
saved by speeding meant something to you or
somebody else.

Maybe we'd feel better if we could imagine that
you were a doctor rushing somewhere to deliver a
baby or ease somebody's pain. The life of our dog
to shorten someone's suffering – that mightn't have
been so bad.

But even though all we saw of you was your
car's black shadow and its jumping tail lights as
you roared down the road, we know too much
about you to believe it.

You saw the dog, you stepped on your brakes,
you felt a thump, you heard a yelp and then my
wife's scream. Your reflexes are good, we know,
because you jumped on the gas again and got out
of there fast.

Whoever you are, mister, and whatever you do
for a living, we know you are a killer.

And in your hands, driving the way you drove
Tuesday night, your car is a murder weapon.

You didn't bother to look, so I'll tell you what

the thump and the yelp were. They were Vicky, a six-months-old Basset puppy; white, with brown and black markings. An aristocrat, with twelve champions among her forebears; but she clowned and she chased, and she loved people and kids and other dogs as much as any mongrel on earth.

I'm sorry you didn't stick around to see the job you did, though a dog dying by the side of the road isn't a very pretty sight. In less than two seconds you and that car of yours transformed a living being that had been beautiful, warm, white, clean, soft and loving into something dirty, ugly, broken and bloody. A poor, shocked and mad thing that tried to sink its teeth into the hand it had nuzzled and licked all its life.

I hope to God that when you hit my dog you had for a moment the sick, dead feeling in the throat and down to the stomach that we have known ever since. And that you feel it whenever you think about speeding down a winding country road again.

Because the next time some eight-year-old boy might be wobbling along on his first bicycle. Or a very little one might wander out past the gate and into the road in the moment it takes his father to bend down to pull a weed out of the driveway, the way my puppy got away from me.

Or maybe you'll be real lucky again, and only kill another dog, and break the heart of another family.

Richard Joseph
Westport, Conn.

THE DOG IS A DREAM OF AN ACTOR
Eric Knight to Jere Knight
8 August 1942

*Life changed for English writer Eric Knight with the
publication of his book* Lassie Come-Home, *adapted
from a short story of his that was previously printed in
American magazine* The Saturday Evening Post. *The
novel told the story of Lassie, a Rough Collie determined to escape her new owner, and was a huge and
instant hit on publication in 1940. In 1943, the book
became a movie. In 1954, it became a television series
that ran for nineteen years. This letter was written by
Knight from Hollywood in 1942, as he excitedly
watched the movie being made. Sadly, months after he
wrote to his wife, Knight was killed in action while
serving as a major in the US Army. He died without
having seen the finished film.*

THE LETTER

Wo, darlint:

Tired as usual, and much too much work to do—
and the amount of it is my honor. You value a
horse by the pounds of load you can pile upon
him, and you never give an ass a horse's load.
Something like that.

If I look at Hollywood dames in white-walled
cars, I think: "What the hell am I in this war for?"
If I look at words in terms of freedom and honor, I
don't have to ask myself any question at all. I know
what I am here for.

News. I just saw some rushes of LASSIE, and
they are exciting. They said they had a lot of
straight dog stuff without acting, and that interested me. They have a really beautiful collie for
Lassie, only (secret) Lassie is really a Laddie and
they hide it very well. The dog is a dream of an
actor. All the footage was rough, not even cut, and
yet you damned near died to see it. They have the
first shots of the escape, and the dog heading down
the road. They took up in Washington magnificent
Scottish shots—all in technicolor—with the dog
starting down from the sea-shore. When you see
the blood from the paws on the sharp rocks, and
the dog swimming a flooded river, and dragging

itself up the bank, and lying down to lick its bleeding paws, and fighting off the shepherds' dogs, you damned near die. It was tricky work, but the black sheep dog that attacks Lassie actually went into the bust-up, and the Lassie dog came back and the villain actually suddenly backed off and slunk away. It's such stuff that you don't even have to have sequence to get a wallop—no sound, no whining, no music.

I met Marx et al, but bowed away immediately, saying: "I am in the army, and I have and can have nothing to do with the picture, but I merely hope from all my heart that you make it dignified—and if you do you'll have a grand film." Marx said after the conference they decided to change not one line of the story, merely leaving out the puppies at the end.

But from the footage and the cast, they're spending a mint on it, and it is to be one of their big production pictures. The crew's been nearly a month just shooting dog-scenes. They don't pay for that unless they really want a good film and believe in the story.

But the dog is a sweet collie, and breaks your heart. And what an actor. But did I scare the pretty pants off them all. It was all silent, and I watched the dog. They said: "You know, no one in the world will ever know how this film was made, because this dog is so wonderful it never looks at the camera or looks at its owner, and just does the things without giving the slightest indication."

So I started talking to the dog, saying: "Come to the edge of the water—stop! Look around! Walk into the water, a little further. Taste it! You don't like it—no! Yes, turn round and come this way. No—walk slower. That's it. Slowly. Stop! Lie down now!"

And the big shots nearly wanted to stop all production.

They said: "Can you see that?"

I said, yes.

"My God," says Marx. "How many people will be able to see that? We thought no one could tell—but that's just exactly what [owner/trainer Rudd Weatherwax] was saying to the dog."

I said that not one person in twenty thousand could tell.

But they insisted on knowing just how I could tell and know when the dog was going to do something else.

I said: "Because I wrote the book—and you don't write a Lassie Come-Home unless you know a collie and the inside of its mind and soul perhaps better than some of the men know the mind and soul of their own wives. I know dogs, that's all."

It was a terrific showoff—but I wouldn't have told them for a thousand dollars. But my God, there was Toots doing what I told her—the hesitant step, the heart-aching trying for swift obedience, and there was the one tip-off that no one but a collie man would ever see. It was—sure, the dog had been trained not to look at the camera. Sure it didn't look at the man. But at every command, nothing could stop the signal, the sudden slight movement of the ear as the dog got the spoken command. Then all I had to say was exactly what new evolution the dog did. "That's right. Stop! Lie down!" Only the flick of the ear to the sound is the tip-off. But I had them worried.

LETTER 26
POOR HAIRY PHANTOM
Jane Welsh Carlyle to Ellen Twisleton
30 November 1855

Born in East Lothian, Scotland, in 1801, Jane Welsh
Carlyle is best known for both her surviving corre-
spondence and her marriage to the essayist and
philosopher Thomas Carlyle. A volume of Carlyle's
letters was once reviewed by Virginia Woolf, who
hailed her as one of the greats. In a number of these
missives can be found mention of Carlyle's dear
Maltese dog, Nero, who lived with the Carlyles for
close to eleven years. There is also this letter, written
in the voice of Nero to Carlyle's Bostonian friend, Ellen
Twisleton, in response to something she had recently
gifted to Carlyle, much to the dog's annoyance.

THE LETTER

5 Cheyne Row Chelsea
30th November / 1855

Stranger Lady!

Please to not think it presuming, that one who is
only a Dog, and a very little one, should write to
you, out of his own head. I am not wanting in
modesty, I do assure you; from earliest puppyhood,
it has been inculcated on me that presumption is as
insufferable in dogs as in men. Even my Master,
tho' calling me "*miserable chimera*"—"*Poor hairy
Phantom*"—and other uncouth names, admits that I
have "a quadruped sense of propriety" and am
"very easily repressed." And if *he* says that of me;
you may think—!

The fact is, Madam, I am in "a state of
mind"—in one of those moments which French
Dogs call SUPRÈME, and in which one does and
may do—anything! Oh Madam; unless I *open my
heart* to someone; I shall go mad—and *bite*! Yes! I
feel myself trembling on the brink of
HYDROPHOBIA!

"But what have *you* to do with me"? you
ask—"you hardly know me, to speak to." Oh
Madam! Madam! you have more to do with me

than you think! It is *you* who have changed me from a trustful loving little Dog, into a Dog chased by Furies! Had you left *that*—*Duck*—that horrible Duck in her native pond—above all if you had not introduced her *here*; I had not been now the rabid thing you see!

For seven years my Mistress and I had been one anothers "first object." Not even the little female Dog at No 10, tho' I own to having shown her some unmeaning gallantries, ever came seriously between us. And now comes this—*Duck*—this creature without heart or bowels! And off goes my mistress into raptures with her—has no eyes but for *her*! It is *she* who gets shown off to visitors—She who is the new favourite—while I unnoticed unpraised look gloomily on—foaming at the mouth with rage!

Madam: it is easier to destroy the peace of Families than to patch it up. Still I implore you— on my hind legs implore you—to try to repair this evil you have unconsciously done, to me a poor little Quadruped, who never harmed you! Inferior animal tho' I am, I can perceive you have "talents to drive the Genii to despair"; turn them to recovering my still dear Mistress from her infatuation—and making her see the infamy of setting up new favourites at the age she is—and the

cruelty of—of— Oh I can write no more—my
heart! my heart!—Wo-o-o-h Wo-o-o-o-h Who o o
oho o o h!

The unfortunate
Nero.

LETTER 27
THE TRUST REPOSED IN YOU WAS SADLY
MISDIRECTED

David McLachan to *The Scottish Fancier and Rural
Gazette*
May 1887

*Established in 1884, The Scottish Fancier and Rural
Gazette was a monthly illustrated journal dedicated to
'The breeding, management, and exhibition of Dogs,
Poultry, Pigeons, Cage Birds, and other Pet Stock'. In
its issue of May 1887, it featured this letter, written by
the disgruntled owner of an Irish terrier who had
recently been exhibited at a dog show in Ayr, Scotland.
It seems from Mr McLachan's amusingly furious
complaint that the judging had not been up to his high
standards.*

THE LETTER

As I was an exhibitor of Irish Terriers at Ayr yesterday, and as I was very much disappointed with the awards, I feel it a duty to demand an explanation from you for acting in the manner you did. In the dog class you gave Garryford first, which was right enough, provided Garryford had a right to be there, which is very doubtful, he being a champion dog. Were it not that Garryford's new owner is a direct descendant of "King Agrippa" he would not have been there, as no gentleman would send a champion dog to compete in such classes. As for Gifford – had it not been that his chain was in Mr Lumsden's left hand, he would not have been looked at, as no man who knows anything about an Irish Terrier would look at him. You gave third to a dog with nothing but legs to look at; whereas Fagan got fourth – a dog that has been first in England before a competent judge. Either you know nothing about an Irish Terrier, or, if you do, it was evident that it was the owner and not the dog, that got the prize.

In the bitch class you placed Randy fourth after being changed from fifth – a bitch that was second at Glasgow in a class of twenty dogs. You put her first at Wishaw and gave nothing to Erin; yesterday you gave Erin second over the same bitch Randy, and made the lame excuse that you did not know Erin – a bitch wide in chest and with a very bad leg, and has a face like a monkey. You told me in the ring that Randy's coat was soft; there was no difference in her coat from Wishaw show. I have bred Fox, Skyes and Irish Terriers before you knew what a dog was. I should like to know how you have the audacity to pose before the public as a judge of Irish Terriers. Did you ever breed or own one? Do you know anything about their points? If you do, the trust reposed in you was sadly misdirected. Do you imagine for a moment that I am going to be sat upon by an amateur like you? I have no objection to other people paying for your education, but I do not intend to do so. I made careful search yesterday after I got my dogs on their benches, for the purpose of having an explanation from you. You may consider yourself very lucky I did not find you – and future exhibitors of Irish Terriers were unfortunate that I did not – as I would have given you a few practical hints that you would have remembered every time you saw an Irish Terrier. However I will make it my special study to see you on the subject. Meantime I demand an explanation from you. I do not intend to speak behind your back, as you did of me in the ring yesterday, but to inform you that I intend to write to the "Stockkeeper" and other papers on the subject.

You told Mr Lumsden yesterday that you had made a mess of it so Mr Lumsden told me. Well, it is my turn now. And explanation I demand at once.

MY DARLING GIRL
Sue Perkins to Pickle
January 2014

In Cheshire, England, in 2002, a mischievous eight-week-old Beagle was carefully lifted from its bed and placed in the hands of its new owner: British comedian and broadcaster Sue Perkins. Thus began a loving relationship that would last for eleven years. Pickle was just two years old when vets discovered a cancerous tumour. Thankfully, its removal was a success. Sadly, when the cancer returned years later it proved terminal. Perkins wrote this letter soon after Pickles closed her eyes for the last time.

THE LETTER

My darling girl,

First, a confession: I had you killed. I planned it
and everything; asked the vet round and a nurse in
a green uniform with white piping – all with the
express intention of ending your life. Yes, I know. I
know you had no idea, because I had been prac-
tising for weeks how to keep it from you, and how
– when that time came – I could stop my chest
from bursting with the fear and horror and unbearable, unbearable pain of it all.

I sat there, in your kitchen (it was always your
kitchen), numb, and filled in a form about what to
do with your remains. I ticked boxes as you lay
wheezing in your sleep on the bed next door. I
made a series of informed, clinical decisions on the
whys and wherefores of that beautiful, familiar
body that had started to so badly let you down.
Then, once the formalities were over, I came in and
did what I've done so many days and nights over
so many months and years. I lay behind you, left
arm wrapped round your battle-scarred chest and
whispered into your ear.

I love you.

So that was my secret. And I kept it from you
until your ribs stopped their heaving and your

legs went limp and your head fell as heavy as grief itself in my arms. Then, when I knew you were no longer listening, I let it out – that raging, raging river of loss. I cried until my skin felt burned and my ears grew tired from the sound of it all.

It wasn't pretty.

OK. Confession over.

Now what you also need to know is that this is NOT a eulogy. Quite frankly, Pickle, you don't deserve one, because, as you are well aware, your behaviour from birth, right up to the bitter end, was unequivocally terrible.

As a pup, you crunched every CD cover in the house for fun. You chewed through electrical cable and telephone wires. You ripped shoes and gobbled plastic. You dived into bins, rolled in shit and licked piss off of pavements. You ate my bedposts.

As an adult you graduated to raiding fridges and picnics, you stole ice cream from the mouths of infants, you jumped onto Christmas tables laden with pudding and cake and blithely walked through them all, inhaling everything in your wake.

You puked on everything decent I ever owned. You never came when called, never followed a path, never observed the Green Cross Code and only sat on command when you could see either a cube of cheese or chicken in my hand (organic, or free range at a push).

And last, but not least, you shat in my bed (yes, I know they were dry and discreet little shits, but they were still shits, you shit).

Here's another thing, while I'm at it. I'm angry. Why? Because you, madam, are a liar. You made me think you were OK. You allowed me to drop you off at our mate Scarlett's farm and leave you there for weeks while I went away working thinking that all was well. Yet it wasn't, was it? The cancer fire was already lit, sweeping through your body, laying waste to it while my back was turned.

I look back at photos sent to me while I was away from you, and I can see it now – that faint dimming of the eyes, the gentle slackening of muscle. The tiniest, tiniest changes in that cashmere fur of yours. It haunts me still. Had I been there, I would have noticed, would I not? Me, your anxious guardian and keeper of eleven and a half years.

I found out about the lump the day I landed. Scarlett rang me with the news as I boarded a train for Willesden Junction. The most momentous moments can come at the most banal. It had just appeared, out of nowhere, as surprising and fast as you, on your neck. You never did anything by halves, and there it was, the size of a lemon, wrapped round your lymph.

I took you home the next day, to Cornwall, the place that we love best, and you allowed me, for a while at least, to believe that nothing was wrong. We rose at sunset, in the light of those Disney-pink skies, and walked the ancient tracks together – before you got bored and veered off, full tilt, in search of the latest scent.

But your lies could only carry you so far before your body gave you away. I saw your chest starting to heave when you took a breath at night. Your bark became hoarse. You no longer tore around the house causing havoc. You were biddable (you were never biddable), you ate slowly (oh, don't be ridiculous).

Yet still, the denial. Forgive me for that. After all, we'd beaten it before, you and I. Twice. Even when the vet told me your lungs were hung with cancerous cobwebs and there was nothing more to be done, I went out and started doing. I sped to the health food store and returned with tinctures and unguents and capsules. And there you were having to eat your precious last dinners covered in the dusty yellow pall of turmeric and a slick of Omega 3s. So silly. So silly, in retrospect. I should have let you eat cake and biscuits and toast and porridge. But I thought I could save you. I really thought I could.

I didn't ever believe that something as alive as you could ever succumb to something as ordinary as death.

After all, how could you be sick when you ran and jumped and played, day after day after day?

And then, I got it. You were doing it all for me. You were dragging yourself into the light, every morning, for me. All of it. For me.

And as fierce and possessive as my love was, I couldn't let you do that any more. You were eighty years old, by human reckoning.

You were eighty years old and you still flew into the boot of the car without assistance (assistance is for old dogs, you didn't know how to be an old dog), you still strode the Heath with that graceful, lupine lope of yours. You skidded round corners, you sniffed and barked and hectored and lived to life's outer margins. On the day you died, you pottered for over an hour in the meadows with the sun on your back, without a care in the world. I am so very grateful for that.

When someone once took a punch at me, you leaped in the air and took it. When I discovered I couldn't have children, you let me use your neck as a hankie. You were my longest relationship, although I think any decent psychologist would have deemed us irredeemably co-dependent. You were the engine of my life, the metronome of my day. You set the pulse and everything and everyone moved to it. What a skill. I woke to your gentle scratch on the door (it wasn't gentle, it was horrific and you have destroyed every door in every house we have lived in – I am just trying to make you sound nice), and the last sound at night was the sound of you crawling under your blanket and giving that big, deep, satisfied sigh.

I have said I love you to many people over many years: friends, family, lovers. Some you liked, some you didn't. But my love for you was different. It filled those spaces that words can't reach.

You were the peg on which I hung all the baggage that couldn't be named. You were the pure, innocent joy of grass and sky and wind and sun. It was a love beyond the limits of patience and sense and commensuration. It was as nonsensical as it was boundless. You alchemist. You nightmare.

Thank you for walking alongside me during the hardest, weirdest, most extreme times of my life, and never loving me less for the poor choices I made and the ridiculous roads I took us down.

Thank you, little Pickle. I love you.

From the four-eyed one who shouted at you,

held you, laughed at you, fed you and, for some
reason utterly unbeknownst to you, put all your
shit in bags.

X

Pickle Perkins

Born: 20-08-02

Skipped to next destination: 14-01-14

'YOU PUKED ON
EVERYTHING DECENT
I EVER OWNED . . .'

— Sue Perkins

Bishop Morris, *Letters from Petrarch*, 1966; permission conveyed through Copyright Clearance Center, Inc.

LETTER 18 from Bob Hope to Fala Roosevelt (1945) from William Robert Faith, *Bob Hope: A Life in Comedy*, Da Capo Press, 2003, Used with permission from The Hachette Book Group.

LETTER 21 from Gertrude Stein to Alexander Woollcott (1935) from Gertrude Stein, *The Letters of Gertrude Stein & Thornton E. Wilder*, Yale University Press, Used with permission from David Higham Associates.

LETTER 23 from Georgia O'Keeffe to Todd Webb (1981) Letter from Center for Creative Photography, University of Arizona. ©Todd Webb Archive. Used with permission from Todd Webb Archive.

LETTER 24 from Richard Joseph to the man who killed his dog (1955) from *The Los Angeles Times*, 27 November 1955, p. 305, Used with permission from Frederick Fell Publishers, Inc., North Bay Village, Florida 33141.

LETTER 25 from Eric Knight to Jere Knight (1942) from Geoff Gehman, *Down But Not Quite Out in Hollow-Weird: A Documentary in Letters of Eric Knight* (The Scarecrow Filmmakers Series):62, Scarecrow Press, 1998, Used with permission from Rowman and Littlefield Publishers, Reproduced with permission of the Licensor through PLSclear.

LETTER 26 from Jane Welsh Carlyle to Ellen Twisleton (1855) from Jane Carlyle, 'Letter to Ellen Twisleton, November 3, 1855,' in *The Collected Letters of Thomas and Jane Welsh Carlyle*, from the Carlyle Letters Online: https://carlylletters.dukepress.edu/volume/30/lt-18551130-N-ETW-01, Used with permission from Duke University Press.

LETTER 28 from Sue Perkins to Pickle, reprinted by kind permission of Sue Perkins.

ACKNOWLEDGEMENTS

It requires a dedicated team of incredibly patient people to bring the Letters of Note books to life, and this page serves as a heartfelt thank you to every single one of them, beginning with my wife, Karina – not just for her emotional support during such stressful times, but for the vital role she has played as Permissions Editor on many of the books in this series. Special mention, also, to my excellent editor at Canongate Books, Hannah Knowles, who has somehow managed to stay focused despite the problems I have continued to throw her way.

Equally sincere thanks to all of the following: Teddy Angert and Jake Liebers, whose research skills have helped make these volumes as strong as they are; Rachel Thorne and Sasmita Sinha for their crucial work on the permissions front; the one and only Jamie Byng, whose vision and enthusiasm for this series has proven invaluable; all at Canongate Books, including but not limited to Rafi Romaya, Kate Gibb, Vicki Rutherford and Leila Cruickshank; my dear family at Letters Live: Jamie, Adam Ackland, Benedict Cumberbatch, Aimie Sullivan, Amelia Richards, and Nick Allott; my agent, Caroline Michel, and everyone else at Peters, Fraser & Dunlop; the many illustrators who have worked on the beautiful covers in this series; the talented performers who have lent their stunning voices not just to Letters Live, but also to the Letters of Note audiobooks; Patti Pirooz; every single archivist and librarian in the world; everyone at Unbound; the team at the Wylie Agency for their assistance and understanding; my foreign publishers for their continued support; and, crucially, my family, for putting up with me during this process.

Finally, and most importantly, thank you to all of the letter writers whose words feature in these books.

131

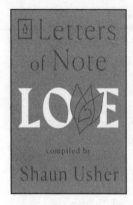 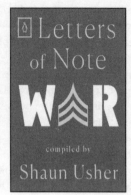